This book
belongs to

~~Edmund Hutton~~.

THE LNER 4-6-0 CLASSES

THE LNER
4-6-0 CLASSES

John F. Clay & J. Cliffe

LONDON

IAN ALLAN LTD

First published 1975

ISBN 0 7110 0622 9 88/74

© Ian Allan Ltd. 1975

Published by Ian Allan Ltd. Shepperton, Surrey and
printed in the United Kingdom by The Press at
Coombelands Ltd., Addlestone, Weybridge, Surrey
KT15 1JN

Contents

Preface

The 4–6–0 locomotives were not the front line troops of the LNER; that position was taken by the Pacifics and 2–6–2s. Nevertheless much valuable work was performed by 4–6–0 locomotives, both of the older pre-grouping designs and later of those built by the LNER. The former Great Eastern and Great Central lines for many years saw nothing larger than 4–6–0 engines. Over 40 years spanned the time between the building of the first passenger 4–6–0 for the North Eastern and the building of the LNER B1 class and during this period many interesting technical changes took place. Although the B1 was not really so very much bigger than the first NER 4–6–0 it was capable of much enhanced performance.

This is not a story of locomotives of sublime perfection—such locomotives never really existed—but of some locomotives of absorbing interest. The real heroes of the story are the men, especially the firemen, who made it possible to include so many examples of excellent running.

By intention performance is given a leading position in the book, while the statistical history has been given in outline only, as the aim has been to be complementary to rather than competitive with other more specialised works.

Considerable help has been given by former Locomotive Inspector P. H. V. Banyard who, after a lifetime spent as fireman, driver and inspector on the GCR, travelled far and wide on locomotive footplates on other railways as a senior inspector. H. A. Gamble, the founder of the Leicester Railway Society, has read the script and made helpful suggestions. Thanks are also due to two distinguished railwaymen. G. J. Aston has kindly lent the priceless Charlewood note books and several logs from these are included as well as a most exciting high-speed run timed by Mr Aston. R. H. N. Hardy has kindly given permission for the use of material from his book *Steam in the Blood* (Ian Allan, 1971) and from his numerous articles.

The Editor of the *Railway Magazine* has given permission for the quotation of performance details and other material from past issues and similar permission has been given by G. Goslin for the use of material from the *Gresley Observer*. Information about the coal consumption of the Caprotti B3s has been given by H. Phillips and P. W. B. Semmens. Various items of interest have been provided by J. D. Cliffe, brother of J. Cliffe, the co-author, by N. Harvey, R. N. Clements, K. R. Phillips, Gp Capt J. N. C. Law, D. H. Landau, P. J. Coster and H. N. James. To all these and to any who, through inefficiency not intent, may have been omitted, a great debt of gratitude is owed. All photographers are thanked for their help, with once again a special word of appreciation for T. G. Hepburn's many fine prints. We are grateful to Peter Winding for preparing the line drawings.

Leicester, May 1974   John F. Clay

London, January 1975   J. Cliffe

CHAPTER ONE

The History of the
4-6-0 Type

The 4–6–0 proved to be one of the most generally useful wheel
arrangements in the whole history of steam. It was used almost
everywhere both for passenger and freight service. It had the
advantage of being able to keep its feet well in starting and during
heavy pulling at low speeds and yet it was a type with a most
distinguished record of high-speed running. Something like 75 per
cent of the adhesion weight of a 4–6–0 was available for adhesion.
It has been suggested that, because the 4–6–0 had coupled wheels
at the rear, the drawbar pull at starting, by concentrating greater
effective weight on the trailing axle, increased adhesion while a
Pacific or Hudson class engine, without equalising beams, lost
adhesion because the pull concentrated extra weight on an idle
carrying axle and reduced the weight on the driving wheels. This
theory has been disputed, but the more effective starts of 4–6–0s
as compared with more powerful Pacifics could be observed everyday in British practice, so that the effect was unquestionable, whatever the reason.

The capacity for clean starts without slipping made it possible
for a designer, if he was so minded, to build 4–6–0 engines with a
tractive effort as great as or greater than contemporary Pacifics.
This led to some confusion among interested amateurs, who thought
that tractive effort must be the qualification of power. They were
encouraged in this belief by the propagandists of certain railways.
The fallacy was an easy one to accept, for many people who watched
trains could not fail to notice the crisp clean starts of 4–6–0s as
compared with the slipping which so often characterised those of
Atlantic or Pacific class locomotives. When it came to the need for
high sustained horsepower at speed, the bigger boilers of the Pacific
type engines gave them an advantage over 4–6–0s. However, the
greater potential capacity of the Pacific could not always be realised
owing to the limitations of hand firing. On test, even some relatively
small 4–6–0s needed two firemen when maximum efforts were
required. A strong case can be made for the contention that on
certain railways, with moderate distances but with peculiar difficulties of curves and gradients, the 4–6–0 was a wiser choice than
a Pacific.

It was a disadvantage of the 4–6–0 that its narrow firebox was of
necessity smaller than the wide firebox of a Pacific. But, in practice,

it would appear that many narrow fireboxes gave excellent evaporation rates for their size. Certain engines of the British LNWR and GWR are cases in point, as are some engines of the French Nord and Paris–Orleans railways. There was, however, some difficulty in locating an ashpan of adequate size owing to the presence of the rear coupled axle. Various methods were employed to minimise this difficulty. The presence of a coupled axle under the cab tended in general to make 4–6–0s less easy riding at high speeds than Pacifics, but there were, of course, individual designs of Pacific which for other reasons were poor riders, while some 4–6–0s had a good reputation. The personal choice of the chief designer, in most cases, governed the proportions of Pacifics and 4–6–0s used on a railway. The LNER, during the reign of Sir Nigel Gresley, was limited in the number of new 4–6–0s by comparison with other contemporary British railways, but during the last few years of the LNER's independent existence events showed that quite likely a different situation would have arisen had the lot fallen elsewhere.

The 4–6–0 type had its beginning in the United States where there was a desire for more adhesion weight than was possible with a 4–4–0 on the rather flimsy track. The first 4–6–0 was built by Septimus Norris in Philadelphia in 1847. It had a Bury type haycock firebox with an axle in front and another behind. It had the contemporary large stack associated with wood burning. A number of similar engines followed in the next few years, all intended for heavy freight service in the mountain area of Pennsylvania.

For many years the role of the 4–6–0 was limited to slow heavy haulage, but gradually mixed traffic types were introduced. In 1895, possibly inspired by the British Races to Scotland, the New York Central group made a fast run from New York to Buffalo, 436½ miles in 407 min. On the earlier sections the traditional American 4–4–0s were used, but for the final stretch from Erie to Buffalo a 4–6–0 mixed traffic engine with 5ft 8in driving wheels was turned out and this proved to be the fastest of all. Engineer Bill Tunkey covered the 86 miles in 70min 46sec and a maximum speed of 92mph was claimed. This run, in contrast to many American claims of the period, seems to be well authenticated. In Britain, in 1895, there were still serious doubts on some railways as to whether the four-coupled engine should replace the single for fast running. Here was a startling vista of the future that lay ahead of the six-coupled express engine.

During the 19th Century the construction of 4–6–0 locomotives in Europe was limited mainly to the field of goods or mixed traffic designs. In Britain 4–6–0 locomotives were built for export overseas before any found their way into service on our own lines. In 1880 Dubs and Co of Glasgow built the first of the Indian State Railways Class L general service 4–6–0s. In *Twenty Locomotive Men* (Ian Allan

1958) C. Hamilton Ellis discusses whether the hand of the Highland's David Jones influenced this design; he had acted as a consultant engineer for a number of foreign railways and the Class L would appear to resemble the Jones family of engines in some respects. The first 4–6–0 to appear on the Continent of Europe was built in Italy in 1884 to the design of Cesare Frescot for the Upper Italian Railway; it was characterised by a very short bogie. The fast running European 4–6–0, however, still lay well in the future.

The Highland Railway in Scotland had the longest and most difficult main-line gradients in Britain. There were steeper main-line banks, but they were not of equal length. To climb a Highland bank by the impetus of a fast run at the foot was out of the question; only hard, continuous slogging could win the day. At first Highland freight traffic was not heavy and it could be handled by passenger engines of moderate size, but as the 1890s dawned the need of something altogether more powerful was becoming apparent and in 1894 it was answered with the first of the famous "Big Goods" class of 4–6–0. This was the first 4–6–0 built for use in Britain and the most powerful engine in the land at the time. Although by name and intention they were a goods engine, in actual fact the Jones 4–6–0 did a fair amount of passenger work on the heavy grades as pilots or alone in charge of relief portions at times of heavy traffic. They were impressive-looking engines for 1894 and happily one is still preserved.

It might well have been that the Highland could have introduced the first British 4–6–0 built solely for passenger service as David Jones followed his "Big Goods" by working on the design of a passenger version of the same engine. Unfortunately he met with a serious accident which led to his retirement in 1896. The partly finished design was modified by his successor Peter Drummond and was introduced in 1900, by which time a 4–6–0 passenger engine had been built by Wilson Worsdell for the North Eastern Railway. This design, for one of the constituent companies of the LNER, will be dealt with in more detail in the next chapter. The Highland passenger 4–6–0s were named after castles; in essentials, they were a larger version of the "Big Goods" with a number of Drummond variations. Like the goods 4–6–0s these engines gave many years of good service to the Highland.

The first 4–6–0 to be built in England was No 36, constructed at Swindon for the GWR in August, 1896. This was entirely a Dean design with the Dean boiler and double frames fully in the traditions of Swindon in those days. The engine was intended solely for goods work, with driving wheels 4ft 6in in diameter. There are no records of any emergency use of the engine on passenger work, but it was able to work a much greater unaided load through the Severn Tunnel than the 0–6–0s. Between 1899 and 1903 the GWR built the

"Krugers", which were intended for the same duties, but which included some unmistakable features of the new CME, George Jackson Churchward. The first of the "Krugers" was a 4–6–0 engine. The boiler was largely experimental with a Belpaire firebox and a combustion chamber. Subsequent engines were built as 2–6–0s and were the forerunners of the "Aberdares", which worked the South Wales coal traffic for many years.

The story of the GWR express classes of 4–6–0, which make the name of Churchward an honoured one wherever the steam locomotive is remembered, is, of course, outside the history of the LNER 4–6–0s. It was, however, a most vital influence on all locomotive practice in this country, because it was Churchward who changed mere locomotive building into a science. Some of the later GWR 4–6–0s were rivals to the LNER Pacifics and some details of their design were incorporated into LNER practice, including some of the later 4–6–0s. In as much as Churchward locomotives influenced LNER practice their history is relevant.

Meanwhile, in the US, the 4–6–0 made further history. Some examples were built with the intention of working the fastest expresses. Among the best and almost certainly the most handsome was the Brooks 4–6–0 of the Lake Shore and Michigan Southern. These were large-wheeled, high-speed locomotives with 6ft 8in driving wheels and one of them ran from Toledo to Elkhart, 133 miles, in 114min. They were, however, the last really high-speed 4–6–0s built in the US, as 2–6–2 and 4–6–2s took over after a short reign by the 4–6–0s. Many 4–6–0s continued to be built for mixed traffic duties. The last class to be built was the G5 class of the Pennsylvania RR, which appeared as late as 1935, intended for heavy local passenger work. Just as the American RRs would build a 0–8–0 tender engine for shunting, so did the Pennsylvania build a 4–6–0 tender engine for the type of work that would have called for a tank engine in Britian. The G5s were the most powerful 4–6–0s ever built, as their grate area of 55.8sq ft and tractive effort of 41300lb exceeded that of the GWR "Kings" both in size and potential power output. The boilers of the G5 type 4–6–0s were similar, but differed in details from those of the classic E6S Atlantics which had marked a turning point in US steam locomotive design.

On the Continent the 4–6–0 took a large but not a dominant share of express work. For many years the Est railway in France used the 4–6–0 to the exclusion of the Pacific. Finally the Est introduced the 4–8–2, skipping the intermediate design of Pacific— only to receive, under SNCF auspices, some Chapelon PO type Pacifics which by virtue of their superior efficiency outclassed them all. The lesson of the Chapelon researches was not lost on other French railways, and before the end of steam some Est and Nord 4–6–0s were modified with Lemaitre blast pipes and enlarged steam passages. The performance was improved but by then the 4–6–0s were only needed occasionally on the hardest bookings.

The most advanced 4–6–0 was designed but never built. This was a Chapelon high-speed 4–6–0 with 7ft 3in driving wheels, a boiler pressure of 310lb/sq in and a fully streamlined casing. The intention was to run at speeds of up to 125mph. The boiler was based on that used with great success on the Chapelon 4–8–0s. It will never be known if the 4–6–0 wheel arrangement would have permitted comfortable riding at over 100mph in continuous everyday running, but the careful French maintenance would have helped. Even had this engine been built it would never have dominated as a larger 4–6–4 design was also prepared for similar speeds. These designs were first considered in 1936, but the general project of a range of high-speed steam locomotives was revived in 1945 at the end of World War 2 with the aim of being ready for service during the years 1950–1970. The post-war series was adapted to changed operating conditions and would have been three-cylinder compounds. The 4–6–0 was not included in the post-war range and the whole steam project was abandoned in favour of electrification.

It was in Germany that the most numerous class of 4–6–0 in the world was built. This was the P8 Class which, between 1906 and 1924, reached the amazing total of 3500 units. They were simple two-cylinder engines with a modest axle loading of 17 tons, which allowed them to run almost anywhere and undertake almost any job. The same general purpose theme spread later to Britain, where large numbers of 4–6–0s of similar size and power were built. After World War 1 Germany had to supply locomotives as reparations to replace those lost during hostilities. So it was that the P8 4–6–0 was found in many countries such as Belgium, Poland and Rumania. Many of these countries received the engines with enthusiasm and they survived into the 1970s. In Poland they were fitted with larger boilers and additional examples were added between 1922 and 1934.

Before World War 1 the Germans also built some high-speed 4–6–0s with driving wheels 6ft 5in in diameter as compared with the 5ft 9in wheels of the mixed traffic P8s. These were Class S10 and there were variations with four cylinders in line, four-cylinder compounds and three-cylinder simples. These were fast engines and one was timed on test at 95mph, but after World War 1 German construction for high speed work was concentrated on Pacifics and 4–6–4s.

The 4–6–0 type was, of course, found in many other lands and no chapter of this kind could ever claim to be complete; a complete review of the 4–6–0 type would need a larger book. The basic truth of 4–6–0 history, however, emerges from this review which, although not complete, is hoped to be representative. The general fact that emerges is that the 4–6–0 found its most popular employment as a mixed-traffic engine, but that it also performed some highly praiseworthy service as a front-line high-speed express locomotive. The British Great Western Railway is perhaps the classic example of a 4–6–0 railway and it was on the GWR that the fastest high-speed running by 4–6–0s was achieved. A strong case can be made for the suggestion that the physical features of the GWR made the 4–6–0 the best choice. The LMS worked a large proportion of its heaviest and fastest trains by 4–6–0 locomotives, only building enough Pacifics to handle the cream of the traffic. The LMS "Royal Scot" class, especially in its rebuilt form, could perhaps be said to have equalled the best of the GWR 4–6–0s for general heavy express work and to have pressed them close in high-speed running. On the LNER there were more Pacifics and 2–6–2 locomotives, with the result that the 4–6–0s took a more secondary role. Opinions may vary as to the wisdom of this policy, but it may perhaps be claimed that the LNER was following the concensus of world practice.

CHAPTER TWO

The North Eastern
4-6-0s

At the Paris Exhibition of 1900 two contrasting British locomotives stood together. One was the Midland single No 2601
Princess of Wales, representing a type which had contributed
much to British railway history but which, in 1900, was already
threatened with extinction by the introduction of the corridor
coach and the dining car. The other was the North Eastern 4–6–0
No 2006, which pointed the way towards a future in which six-
coupled express engines would be used in increasing numbers
to solve the problem of increasing loads. No 2006 was awarded
a Gold Medal at the Exhibition and it carried replicas on its
splashers until painted black during World War 1. Before the
1925 Centenary Procession at Darlington, No 2006 was painted
in LNER green and the gold medal replicas were restored.

The Exhibition engine was not the pioneer of the class, as No 2001
had appeared in 1899. Although the NER 4–6–0 was the heaviest
locomotive which had, up till then, been built for passenger
service, it was not really a large engine in basic dimensions. The
grate area of 23sq ft was actually smaller than the 24.5sq ft of the
Midland single. The adhesion weight of the 4–6–0 was, however,
46½ tons against 19 tons of the single, and it was well in excess of
any contemporary British four-coupled engines. The pioneer
engine had a total wheelbase of 48ft 4¾in in order to fit 50ft turntables; this could only be done by reducing the length of the footplate, hence the first three NER 4–6–0s had a shortened cab
with a single side window, whereas the later examples from 2004
onwards, including the Exhibition engine, had the usual large two
window cabs of T. W. Worsdell's design. The NER cabs introduced
by T. W. Worsdell gave excellent protection from the weather,
but they were not immune to criticism on other aspects of their
design. The same general design of cab was continued by Wilson
Worsdell, the designer of the first NER 4–6–0s, and by Vincent
Raven.

The first 4–6–0s were, of course, built before the days of
superheating and originally they carried a boiler pressure of
200 lb/sq in. When new, the centre pair of driving wheels had no
flanges, but this caused trouble and later flanged wheels were
substituted. The cylinders were 20in in diameter with 26in stroke
and the first five had slide valves, but later examples had piston

valves, all driven by Stephenson's link motion. The first ten were built in 1899–1900, followed by another ten in 1906. They were still regarded as express passenger engines and were painted passenger green, but an additional twenty built between June, 1908 and March, 1909 were officially described as intended for fast goods working. The later engines had modified splashers. Before the North Eastern became part of the LNER the whole class had been painted black and regarded as goods engines. At the time these engines were built, a driving wheel diameter of 6ft 1in was considered too small for express work, except perhaps over very heavily graded lines. The NER had little excessive grading on its main line.

At first there seems to have been every intention of giving the 4-6-0 design a good chance to prove itself on the main line and a test run was made between Newcastle and Edinburgh with a load of 352 tons. This consisted of 25 six-wheeled coaches, which would have offered higher running resistance than the equivalent weight in bogie coaches. In fact, although the run was made to the contemporary timings of the "Flying Scotsman", it was really more of a demonstration of the engine's suitability for fast goods or excursion train haulage. No very high speeds were attained anywhere and although C. Rous Marten, who timed the run by official invitation, described the uphill work as "excellent", there was nothing that could not have been equalled by the NER Class R 4-4-0s which had been built at much the same time. The horsepower involved in this test run was, in fact, little higher than would be expected from the Midland single which stood next to the 4-6-0 at the Paris Exhibition, but the 4-6-0 would of course have proved better than any single when used on heavy, relatively slow, trains.

The first NER 4-6-0s paid the price for being pioneers of their type in England. Many of the difficulties that were experienced with these engines were solved as the 4-6-0 was developed. The first NER engines did not exploit the wheel arrangement to its fullest extent and it would have needed rare extra-sensory perception to have looked at No 2001 and seen a "King" or a "Converted Scot" emerging. One of the greatest weaknesses was the fire grate, which was shallow and allowed insufficient air to reach the fire. There were also mechanical defects which caused the class to be driven gently and even the official trial run was hampered by an over-heated eccentric. At first there was some intention to use the 4-6-0s on main line expresses, but before long they found their main role on express freight, with occasional appearances on relief portions of expresses or on the Scarborough excursions. This process was accelerated by the success of the Class R 4-4-0s and by the adoption of the Atlantic type as the front-line express engine.

The original NER 4-6-0s were known as Class S in the NER

locomotive classification. They all eventually received superheated boilers when their pressure was dropped to 160lb/sq in. They never had Gresley snifting valves or Ross Pop safety valves.

A number of experiments were made with engines of this class. No 2003 had Younghusband's patent valve gear and after returning from the Paris Exhibition No 2006 was fitted to burn liquid fuel. Nos 2009 and 2010 were the first engines lined out in gold to work the royal train with the Prince of Wales, later King Edward VII, between York and Newcastle in 1900. The final ten engines had variable blast pipes. The earlier engines had tenders of 3700 gallon capacity, while later ones were given 3940 gallon tenders; the earlier engines subsequently exchanged tenders to conform. The large cab overhung the coupled wheelbase and was wider than that of many 4–6–0s with driving wheel splashers inside the cab.

The first ten engines were built at Gateshead and the second ten at Darlington. The slightly modified engines built in 1907–9 were all constructed at Gateshead and were officially classified S/07, but they never carried the classification on the buffer beam. The entire class of 40 survived to enter LNER stock in 1923 as Class B13 although by then they had degenerated to secondary duties. No 2006 had its moment of glory in the Centenary Procession at Darlington in 1925, but withdrawal started in 1928 and the last engine was taken out of traffic in May, 1937. No 761 was transferred to Departmental stock in 1934.

A strange role was intended for No 761. In September, 1934 the engine was transferred to the Chief Mechanical Engineer's Department at North Road Works, Darlington, for use as a counter-pressure locomotive with the dynamometer car. The aim was to allow an engine under test to run at constant speed uphill and down. To this end, the counter-pressure locomotive was coupled behind the dynamometer car. It assisted the locomotive on test to accelerate to the required speed, but was then put in reverse. Cooling water was now sprayed into the cylinders and steam supplied to the base of the blastpipe to be sucked into the cylinders; this produced resistance and the cooling water was needed to take away the heat generated. With the engine in full reverse gear up to 1500hp could be absorbed. This method of testing was employed in France and a photograph of the LNER 2–8–2 *Cock o' the North* coupled to three brake locomotives is published in *Chapelon, Genius of French Steam*, by Col. H. C. B. Rogers (Ian Allan 1972).

No 761 had some limited service in LNER days and under the 1946 re-numbering it became No 1699. In July, 1948 it was transferred to the newly opened Rugby Testing Plant, but it remained tucked away in a shed, already outclassed by the development of the electric testing units. In May, 1951 it was photographed and then sent to Crewe for scrapping. The excellent external condition of the engine in the published photograph suggested that it had been treated with some care, but the cleaning had been carried out by a volunteer squad of the younger Test Plant engineers during their own time on the previous evening and its glistening brasswork was a shock to authority.

The North Eastern built five express 4–6–os similar in general design to the 2001 class, but with 6ft 8¼in driving wheels. The boiler was slightly different, being 10½in longer but with fewer tubes, though the basic significant dimensions were similar. At first the boiler pressure was 200 lb/sq in, but when superheated this dropped to 175 lb, higher than the 160 lb of the 6ft 1in engines. The first one is variously described as being built in December, 1900 or January, 1901; most likely it was actually built in 1900, but officially entered traffic at the beginning of the new year. They were painted passenger green but became black during the 1914–18 war; however, as they were still considered to be express engines they eventually reverted to passenger green. All five entered LNER stock, but were withdrawn between June, 1929 and May, 1931. They were classified as S1 during NER days and became LNER Class B14.

Certain initial features of design, which had not given satisfaction in Class S, were abandoned in the S1s from the start. The centre pair of S1 driving wheels had flanges and the whole class had Smith piston valves. Although these piston valves pointed the way to future progress, the initial results were not always the equal of the best from the slide valve engines.

The Class S1, however, immediately proved to be reasonably fast by contemporary standards. C. Rous Marten was very favourably impressed by some of his early timings, which were better than his early experiences with the Class V Atlantics. On one of these, with a load of 300 tons, a time of 66min 23sec or 63min net was recorded over the 66·9 miles from Newcastle to Berwick with a maximum of 80mph down 1 in 200 and a minimum of 52½mph up 1 in 170. On another occasion one of the S1s ran a 260 ton train from Darlington to a stop outside York, 43·9 miles, in 40min 51sec start to stop. Good as these runs were neither was beyond the powers of a Class R 4–4–0, but at least it had been proved that six-coupled wheels did not prevent high speeds.

At first the S1s did quite a lot of first-class express work, but as the Atlantics were multiplied they descended to second portions and excursion work. In LNER days they were looked upon as engines to be classed with the mixed traffic types rather than with the express engines. Their history is similar to that of the Manson 4–6–os of the G&SWR, which also did some good work for Rous Marten in their early days but had deteriorated by the time they entered LMS stock.

The multiplication of the Atlantics for frontline express duty on the NER marked a decline in the fortunes of the 4–6–0. It was not, however, comparing like with like, as the Class V Atlantics had a much larger boiler and firebox than the 4–6–0s. The Atlantic wheel arrangement lent itself more easily to the accommodation of a large fire grate with an adequate ashpan. The Great Western tested both Atlantics and 4–6–0s and decided on the six-coupled engines, and the success of the Swindon locomotives suggests that the NER decision was not necessarily a wise one. The facts are that, apart from the five S1s, the NER built 4–6–0s only for mixed traffic duties.

When Vincent Raven had taken over at Darlington he introduced Class S2 which were, in effect, the Class S engines fitted with larger boilers. The new boiler was of 5ft 6in in diameter against 4ft 9in of the originals. The first engine was built in December, 1911. Superheating was introduced from the start and boiler pressure was 180 lb/sq in; the grate area remained at 23·7sq ft. The first six were painted green but later all were painted black.

As mixed traffic engines they were at first given duties which really meant mixed traffic working, such as running one way with a passenger train and returning on a freight. It was assumed that only engines with wheels of limited diameter could do this, but the GNR not many years earlier had been using Stirling and Ivatt singles on Grimsby fish trains. It was the adhesion weight, not the size of the driving wheels, that governed the load which could be started. The S2s were credited with the ability to haul 80 wagons between Darlington and York and 50 wagons between Darlington and Newcastle.

The S2 class was chosen for some experimental modifications. One of the class, No 788, was fitted with a Weir feed pump, which was claimed to introduce water into the boiler at a higher temperature and free from impurities. The last member of the class to be built, No 825, was fitted with Stumpf Uniflow cylinders. The idea of the Uniflow engine was almost as old as steam, but it had its main application in stationary engine practice. The idea was that, if steam could be exhausted at the centre of the cylinder instead of having to retrace its path pushed by the steam in the other end of the cylinder, there would be less loss of efficiency resulting from the cooling of cylinder walls by the exhaust steam. An economy of 5–10 per cent had been observed in stationary engine practice.

The Stumpf arrangement as applied to No 825 involved very long outside cylinders double the length of those on the standard engines. The piston stroke was, however, the same; the extra length was due to a hollow piston half the length of the cylinder. The valves were driven by Walschaerts gear. At starting, the valves allowed steam to exhaust through the admission ports in the normal way, but as cut off was reduced the central ports were uncovered and the exhaust escaped through them. The ports were large and the blast was explosive.

The extra large cylinders were blatantly exposed in No 825 and the engine contrasted with the normal neat outline of NER engines. It was nicknamed "Old Stumpy". A few years later a Class Z Atlantic was also fitted with Uniflow cylinders, but in this case they were tucked away discreetly and only those familiar with loco-motives ever recognised it as anything different.

There is little evidence that the Uniflow engines effected any worthwhile economy. The test results followed the normal pattern of the unconventional [engine; there was a small but hardly significant economy under test conditions, but the practical men—drivers, firemen and locomotive inspectors who bore the heat and burden of the day under everyday working—were less than en-thusiastic. The test results are of some interest, however, for the light they shed on the conventional S2. The NER 4–6–os all had a reputation for heavy coal consumption, but the test figures show little significant difference from those of other pre-Churchward designs on other railways when used on comparative duties. On passenger service with trains of 340 tons at 51·8mph the standard engine burned 4·6 lb per dbhp/hr while the Uniflow engine burned 4·0 lb. On goods trains of more than double the weight but less than half the speed the figure was 3·28 lb for the Uniflow and 3·26 lb for the standard engine. These results did not show any significant difference and such difference as there was lay within the limits or testing error. The apparently better result on freight service was due to the fact that with a heavy load at low speed a higher proportion of the total power was available at the drawbar. Test results over different roads at different speeds are not directly comparable, and in any case broad general conclusions rather than hair-splitting contentious are all that can be justified.

We may conclude that:—

1. The Uniflow system did not show sufficient economy to justify its adoption.
2. The standard S2 was burning coal at a rate of 30 per cent above that of a rationally designed engine with long lap, long travel valves built in the Churchward manner, but it was not sig-nificantly better or worse than the majority of its contemporaries on other lines.

When first built the S2s took a large share of express work, but as more Atlantics were built they reverted to the same duties as the earlier 4–6–os. The whole class entered LNER stock and No 825 was rebuilt with conventional cylinders in 1924. The first examples were withdrawn in September, 1937 and withdrawal was complete in December 1947, the war having doubtless lengthened the lives of some S2s. They became LNER Class B15.

After World War I there was a need for more powerful goods and mixed traffic engines and Sir Vincent Raven, who had returned to the NER knighted for his services to the Government, built the first engines of Class S3. They were officially described as "Goods Engines", but in effect were every bit as fast as Classes S and S2. Although they had smaller driving wheels of 5ft 8in diameter the use of three cylinders, all driving on the front axle, gave excellent balancing, which probably made them just as fast as the two-cylinder 4–6–0s with 6ft 1in wheels.

The use of three sets of Stephensons Link motion with six eccentrics sharing the leading axle with the inside crank webs made things a little crowded. A fly that strayed down into that region while the engine was in motion would have stood a good chance of being hit by something. The three cylinders of 18½in diameter and 26in stroke were served by outside admission piston valves in a common steam chest. The tractive effort of 30032 lb was useful in starting heavy loads and it was backed by a 27sq ft grate. The S3 class was significantly more powerful than earlier NER 4–6–0s.

There was plenty of work for the S3 class on the NER. They were normally on freight trains during the week, but on summer Saturdays and Sundays they would be employed in large numbers on excursion trains to Scarborough or Bridlington. At times they were also turned out on relief portions to main line expresses. In LNER days they strayed south on the GNR and GCR main lines.

The S3s had a reputation for heavy coal burning and shared the nickname "Miners' Friend" with certain other classes. On the GCR they gained the name of "Blood Spitters" on account of the tongue of flame that could be seen above their chimneys when working hard up a bank. Neither official test results nor coal-per-mile figures are available to prove or deny the justice of these names.

At the time of grouping 38 engines entered LNER stock, becoming LNER Class B16, and all had been built at Darlington works. The LNER built 32 more in 1923 and early in 1924, for Gresley allowed more latitude in the building of engines of other designers than did the LMS engineers during the same period. The S3 was of similar size and power to the GNR 2–6–0s of LNER Class K3, but the NER S3 4–6–0s had an edge over the GNR engines on account of their smoother riding, an advantage which was shared with the GCR 4–6–0s of Class B7. A number of small modifications were made to the class in LNER days and two variants were produced by major rebuilding, which will be dealt with in a later chapter.

The NER 4–6–0s were in the main secondary locomotives, for in its main-line policy the NER, like its partners the GNR and the NBR, was an Atlantic line. The main line of the NER was suitable for Atlantics and they managed quite well with heavy loads. It may be argued that on NBR metals, over which NER engines regularly worked, the 1 in 96 of Cockburnspath bank would have been better negotiated by powerful 4–6–0s, and there were secondary routes such as Leeds–Harrogate–Ripon where six coupled wheels could have been an advantage. But arguments as to the superiority of the Atlantic in freer running and in permitting an easier location of an adequate ashpan are not easily sustained in face of the record of the GWR 4–6–0s. The NER 4–6–0s were not, perhaps, the most successful of their type but some useful pioneer work had been done on the NER. The 4–6–0s were good-looking locomotives on a line of good-looking engines and they filled their secondary role adequately.

CHAPTER THREE

The Great Eastern
4-6-0s

The Great Eastern was the only railway to come into the LNER group which had chosen to make the 4-6-0 its main express type and of all the 4-6-0s that the LNER inherited, the GER examples were almost certainly the most successful. The GER 4-6-0s were far from being the largest examples of their type to enter LNER service—there were, in fact, some 4-4-0 designs equally big in basic dimensions—for the GER was a railway with peculiar difficulties and restrictions, and its 4-6-0 locomotives had to be tailored to fit the road.

It is a mistaken belief, frequently expressed by those whose knowledge is limited to areas further west, that all the eastern part of England is flat and therefore that the railways must be level. In reality there are a number of quite steep gradients on the GER main line which, even if relatively short, made the lives of engine crews, working loads heavy in relation to the size of their engines, something less than slippered ease. In the early years of the 20th Century the criterion of all that was best in GER operating was "The Norfolk Coast Express", which had a load of from 350 to 430 tons and was worked non-stop from Liverpool Street to North Walsham 130 miles in 158min by a 50 ton 4-4-0 of the original "Claud Hamilton" 4-4-0 class. Such performance was made possible by using picked locomotives, picked men and picked coal, but the need for a more powerful engine was obvious to all.

As the second decade of the 20th Century began, attention of locomotive engineers was directed towards superheating, which had come in timely manner to give a further lease of life to the steam locomotive. The success of superheating was, at that time, being demonstrated in dramatic fashion by the "George the Fifth" class 4-4-0s of the LNWR. The GER needed an engine of much the same power, but they could not build a 4-4-0 as the axle loading would need to be more than that permitted by the Civil Engineer. The solution was a relatively small, superheated, inside-cylinder 4-6-0.

The first engine, No 1500, appeared early in 1912 during the short period of office of S. D. Holden, son of J. Holden who built the "Claud Hamilton" 4-4-0s. It is thought that S. D. Holden had left the design to the "back room boys" of the period, notably F. V. Russell, Outdoor Assistant to the Locomotive Superintendent, to A. J. Hill, who later succeeded S. D. Holden in the chief position, and to E. S. Tiddeman, Chief Draughtsman. The design was, in effect the boiler and cylinders of a large 4–4–0 fitted into the frames and wheels of a 4–6–0.

The GER designers were faced with extreme limitations of space and weight. The maximum height allowed was 12ft 11in and the width was limited to 8ft 8in, while the adhesion weight of 44 tons spread over three axles was not at all excessive. A problem with the design of any 4–6–0 was the location of the firebox with its ash-pan in relation to the driving axles. Most frequently the firebox was placed between the two rear pairs of driving wheels, as was the case with the NER 4–6–0s. The LNWR 4–6–0s of the "Experiment" and "Prince of Wales" classes had a flat grate extending over the two rear axles, but in the case of the GER 4–6–0s there was a grate flat at the rear but sloping at the front to a point below the level of the middle axle. This meant that the whole grate was further forward than that of the LNWR engines and the price that had to be paid was a fire-hole a long way from the tender.

There was also a benefit in the long space between fire-hole and tender, as the space could be filled by a long, commodious cab which gave excellent shelter from the weather, though on the 1500s there was a disadvantage that a lot of space was taken up by the splashers being inside instead of forward, as was the case with the NER 4–6–0s. The effective working space for the crew was not as great as might have been thought by an observer on the platform watching the GER engine and constrasting its big cab with the exiguous shelters of the GWR 4–6–0s. Men were, however, adaptable and they soon developed a technique of firing which mastered the difficulties. The 1500s were given specially long shovels and firemen learned the best way of placing the coal on the long almost level grate.

There was a tradition of high class enginemanship on the GER, or the 4–4–0 "Claud Hamiltons" could never have coped with the work that they did, and it is significant that the first of the new six-coupled engines was given to Arthur Cage, one of the most successful of the Ipswich drivers who worked the "Norfolk Coast Express". The engines rode well and steamed freely when the proper technique had been mastered and in time there was a standard of running with the 1500s quite as good size for size as that established by the "Clauds". The best work of all was, however, to come in LNER days.

The grate area was 26.5sq ft, a valuable asset in a small boiler worked hard. The cylinders were 20in in diameter with the long stroke, for an engine with inside cylinders, of 28in. There were some doubts as to the wisdom of so long a stroke on inside-cylinder engines needing inside cranks with a 14in throw, but no undue trouble from this seems to have afflicted the 1500s. The valves were above the cylinders and were driven by Stephensons Link motion controlled by a reversing screw with a fine thread, which made it easy for a skilled driver to make frequent adjustments of cut-off to meet the needs of the short ups and downs of some of the GER main lines. As originally built, the 1500s had the broad Schmidt piston valve rings which were steam tight at first, giving good performance, but which soon deteriorated in service with trouble from leakage and failure. These troubles were also shared by the LNWR, whose contemporary superheated locomotives gave brilliant performances at first, but whose coal consumption increased considerably as mileage built up.

The GER 1500s were comparatively light locomotives, built to fit into an exacting set of limits of space and weight, and this meant that there was no room for really large bearing surfaces. The first five had the conventional crank arrangement with the connecting rod cranks and the coupling rod cranks set at 180 deg. to one another. It was found that these engines frequently suffered from overheating in their coupled axle boxes, especially those of the leading, driving, axle. After a few months they were altered to the Stroudley arrangement where the two cranks revolved in unison. This caused a reduction in stresses and less trouble from over-heated axleboxes, and subsequent engines were built to conform. There are, however, few presents of something for nothing in engineering and what seemed like the elimination of one trouble proved to be the transfer of another. A number of fractures of crank pins near the inside web developed. This was countered by the replacement of the original solid crank axles with circular webs by built up cranks with oval webs. New pins of specially toughened molydenum steel were introduced at the same time. These alterations were made in 1924–5 in LNER days. Had there been room right from the start to have built everything bigger and heavier these troubles could have been lessened.

The 1500s were built in the early days of superheating and there was trouble from leakage at the joints where the superheater elements joined the header. This was due to rapid deterioration of the copper and asbestos washers and it allowed steam to escape into the smokebox instead of working its way through the cylinders. Steam was of no value in the wrong place and it reduced the smokebox vacuum, so that the draught was inferior, making it more difficult to generate extra steam to replace that being wasted. The original anti-vacuum valves were connected with the header by an extension piece. The joints on the header were liable to blow and when repair was faced there were studs and set screws in positions of monumental inaccessibility. If a repair hit additional trouble through, for example, a stud breaking off and having to be drilled out, then so much ironmongery had to be removed to get at the job that an engine might be in the shed for a week.

The 1500s were not, of course, alone in having to face mechanical troubles which went hand in hand with the advantages of superheating. There was much to be admired in this GER design, but at all times the need to adapt to a restricted route was the overriding factor. Although the driving axles were as near together as possible there were fears that the engine would prove too long for some of the curves. Some lateral movement was allowed to the rear axle, with spring controlled side play in the axle boxes and spherical bushes at both ends of the rear section of the coupling rods to permit it. This feature was not retained throughout the 1500s' history. The Westinghouse donkey pump provided air for a number of auxiliary purposes, such as sanding, and operated the water scoop. The Westinghouse Co strongly disapproved, with the result that the reservoir was divided into two halves with a non-return valve to preserve the integrity of the brake portion.

The short GER-type tender was fitted, giving a total engine and tender length of 48ft 3in, which allowed 1500s to use 50ft turntables. The front plate of the tender could be lifted out and the fireman could enter the tender to pull coal forward at the end of a long, hard run without the dangerous climbing which caused accidents elsewhere.

The GER 1500s shared the honour of being the most successful of inside-cylinder British 4-6-0s with the LNWR "Princes", but the appearance was altogether different. The black utilitarian appearance of the LNWR engines contrasted with the ornate elegance of the GER machines. The neat lines of the "Claud Hamiltons" had been followed and enlarged upon; the copper-capped chimney and brass beadings to the junctions of smokebox and boiler barrel, safety valve covers, cab windows, main splashers and round the five apertures in the coupling rod splashers all contrasted in dramatic fashion with the royal blue livery. As first built in GER colours, the 1500s were perhaps the nearest thing on rails to the ornate finish of the contemporary showmans' steam road locomotives, many of which were built in the town of Thetford in GER territory.

It was not long before the new engines showed their mettle. In 1912 there was an experimental run with the Hook of Holland boat train set weighing 331 tons. This load was taken by No 1500 from Liverpool Street to Parkeston Quay, 69 miles, in 75min, topping Brentwood Bank at a minimum speed of 46mph. The result was a reduction from 87 to 82min of the daily schedule from Liverpool Street to Parkeston Quay. It became the normal practice for the boat train to pass Shenfield with its 1500 in 26 or 27min against 29–30min with the 4-4-0 "Claud Hamiltons". It is on record that during the pre-war period a 1500 reached Parkeston Quay on time in 82min with a load of 440 tons, while another brought a 500 ton load up from Ipswich, 68 miles, in 86 min.

The increased power of the 4-6-0s made possible some of the sharp bookings planned in the "Radical Alterations" introduced by the progressive American General Manager, H.W., later Sir Henry, Thornton, who took over in May 1914. In the autumn of that year Thornton planned the most comprehensive programme of improved timings ever put into force at one stroke, up till then, on a British railway. The timings were based on the assumption that they could be kept by a 1500 with 15 bogies and by a "Claud" with 12 bogies (the GER corridor bogie coaches were relatively light, averaging about 26½ tons each). The war finally caused the abandonment of Thornton's timetable, but had peace remained there is little doubt that, with minor adjustments, it could have been operated with success.

It is unfortunate that the late Cecil J. Allen, then a young man employed by the GER, was not invited to travel on some of the initial test runs of the 1500s, but he was able to record a run on the "Norfolk Coast Express" with a load of 12 bogies and a six-wheeler totalling 360 tons gross. No 1502 took this load through Shenfield in 27min 56sec, or in 2½-3½min less than Allen's previous best with "Claud Hamilton" class engines. The 130·1 miles to North Walsham were completed in 153min 9sec, or in 150min net. The new 4-6-0 had shown a complete mastery over the task, which demanded the 4-4-0s to be fully extended. This experienced recorder was, however, destined to log his best work by the 1500s during LNER ownership between the wars.

The 1500s were admirably suited for the work on GER and they all entered LNER ownership except No 1506, which was scrapped after the Colchester accident of 1913, being too badly damaged to repair. Becoming Class B12 in the LNER classification, they were well thought of by the LNER authorities and further examples were built. Many minor modifications and a major rebuilding lay ahead of the class. No GER 4-6-0 was named. They have frequently been known as GER Class S69 and the classification has by usage been accepted, but S69 was really only the batch number of the first five engines.

CHAPTER FOUR

The Great Central
4-6-0s

Ninety 4–6–0 locomotives of Great Central design appeared in LNER stock and ten of these were built after the grouping. This total number was greater than the 70 which came from the Great Eastern, but less than the North Eastern total.

Whereas the 70 Great Eastern engines were of one class, the 90 Great Central 4–6–0s came from nine different classes. The GCR made a valiant effort to build a successful 4–6–0, but when history could be told it emerged that the four-coupled designs dominated the high-speed services. The 4–6–0s, however, did a good deal of very useful work on the GC and very possibly earned more money than the high-speed engines. There has been a tendency, perhaps, to dismiss the 4–6–0s in cavalier fashion as being of little merit and it is hoped to show that this was an unduly extreme viewpoint.

The first class of 4–6–0 to be built for the GCR was introduced in 1902. They were known as Class 8 and had a similar boiler to that of the 0–8–0s introduced at the same time for mineral trains. The 4–6–0s were intended for mixed traffic duties. Although almost the same, the boiler of the 4–6–0 differed from that of the 0–8–0 in having a firebox slightly less deep in order to clear the rear axle; this meant a firebox heating surface of 130sq ft, against 140sq ft in the eight-coupled engines. The leading dimensions of the Class 8 4–6–0s were very similar to those of the NER Class S1s, the pioneer British passenger 4–6–0s, but the GC engines were slightly heavier, weighing without tender 65 tons against 62 tons. It was the usual practice of J. G. Robinson to build his engines solidly and they lasted well. The Class 8s were used on the fast fish trains from Grimsby, a service which the GCR viewed with enthusiasm in those days, and the new 4–6–0s soon became known as "The Fish Engines".

As originally built, in saturated form, they were good-looking engines. They were finished in black with red and white lining and photographs of them which survive from the days when engines were cleaned show how attractive a black engine could be. They carried jacks on the running plate at the forward end. At first they had 3250 gallon tenders, but later 4000 gallon tenders. Their driving wheels of 6ft 1in diameter should have given them a full range of action and they did some work on passenger trains including the expresses, but no published record of any exceptional running

Top: NER Class S 4–6–0 No 2002 in original condition with slide valves and single-side-window cab. *Locomotive Publishing Co.*

Centre: No 2002 in LNER days with piston valves and double-side-window cab at Annesley shed. *T. G. Hepburn*

Above: Class B13 No 759 at Scarborough shed. This is one of the later series with modified splashers. *T. G. Hepburn*

Top: The last of the B13s, No 1699, used as a brake locomotive for testing purposes. Photographed at Rugby Test Plant before going to Crewe for scrapping March 22, 1951. *Ian Allan Library*

Centre: North Eastern Class S1 4–6–0 No 2111. *Locomotive Publishing Co.*

Above: No 2112 of Class S1 passing Beningbrough on an up express. *Locomotive Publishing Co.*

Top right: NER Class S2 4–6–0 No 825 fitted with Stumpf Uniflow cylinders. *Locomotive Publishing Co.*

Right: S2 No 825, the Stumpf Uniflow engine, working the 12.30pm Newcastle–Liverpool express. *Cecil J. Allen Collection*

Top: Class S2 No 815 as LNER Class B15 at York Shed. *T. G. Hepburn*

Above: NER Class S3, LNER Class B16/1 No 61410 at Scarborough Shed. *T. G. Hepburn*.

Below: Class B16/1 No 61470 restarting the 12.42pm Leeds – Scarborough from its stop at Seamer Junction on July 21, 1958. *M. Mensing*

Top: Class B16/2 No 61475 at York, May 23, 1953. *J. Robertson*

Above: B16/3 No 61418 at York in July 1962; the reversing rod on the left
hand side provides the easiest identification of this class as compared
with B16/2. *A. W. Martin*

Below: Class B16/3 Thompson rebuild No 61420 on Scarborough–Leicester
Special at Leicester GCR in August, 1952. *J. F. Clay*

Above: GER 1500 Class 4–6–0 No 1515 passing Chadwell Heath with the "Norfolk Coast Express". *Locomotive Publishing Co.*

Below: GER 4–6–0 No 1528 leaving Ipswich on a down express. *The late Cecil J. Allen*

Top right: Class B12 No 8509 experimentally fitted with the Dabeg Feed Water Heater. *Locomotive Publishing Co.*

Centre right: Class B12 No 8569 at Norwich. *T. G. Hepburn*

Bottom right: Class B12 No 8523 fitted with ACFI feed water heater at Norwich. *T. G. Hepburn*

Top: Class B12 No 8533 ascending Brentwood Bank with the down "Day Continental". *F. R. Hebron*

Above: Class B12 2 No 8580, fitted with Lentz poppet valves, near Romford with the down "Day Continental". *F. R. Hebron*

Top: Class B12 No 8572 with its Lentz valves replaced by piston valves in the 1930s, photographed at Stratford Shed. *T. G. Hepburn*

Above: Class B12/4 with small round-top boiler on train from Elgin at Aberdeen, April 15, 1949. *J. F. Henton*

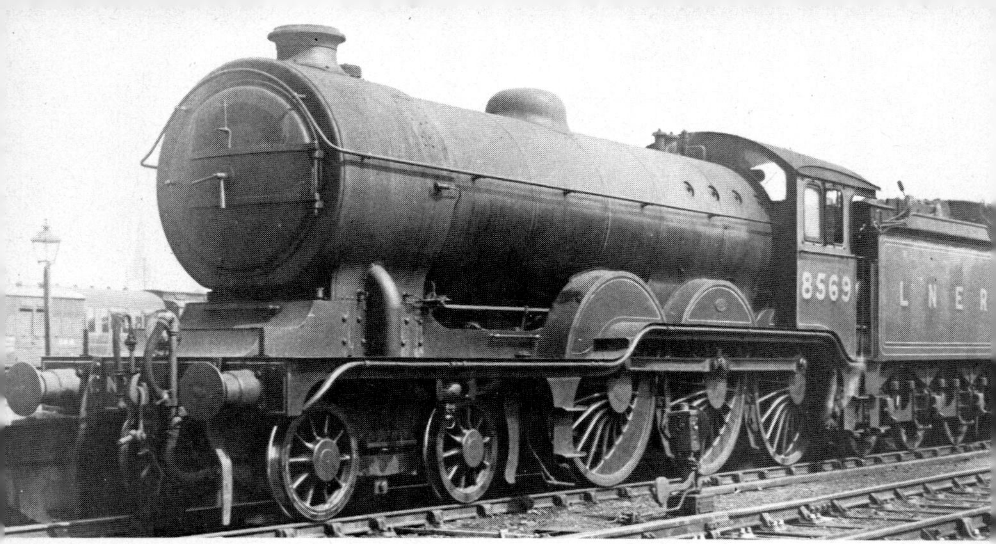
8569
L N E R

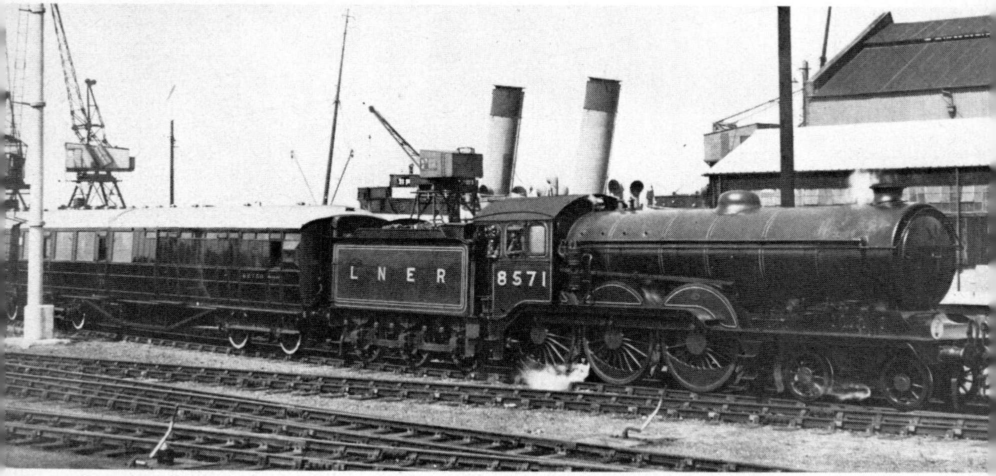
L N E R
8571

L N E R
1577

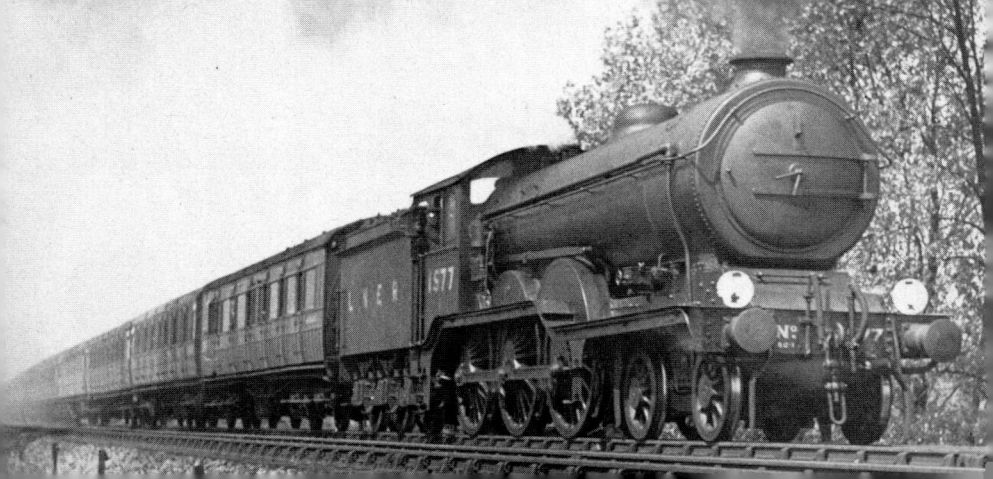

Top left: Class B12/3 No 8569 at Yarmouth. *T. G. Hepburn*

Centre left: Class B12/3 No 8571 on the "Hook of Holland Boat Train" at Harwich Parkeston Quay. *Ian Allan Library*

Bottom left: Class B12/3 in LNER black on down Norwich restaurant car express climbing out of Colchester on May 22, 1948 towards Parsons Heath Box. *C. W. Footer*

Above: Class B12/3 No 61565 in early BR livery leaving Grantham on stopping train to Peterborough. *T. G. Hepburn*

Below: Class B12/3 No 61572 crossing from up main to goods line at Cambridge North on its last main line run on a Swaffham–Liverpool Street special on May 16, 1961. *G. D. King*

Above: GCR "Fish Engine" No 1067 in GCR black livery at Nottingham Victoria. *T. G. Hepburn*

Below: LNER Class B9 goods 4–6–0 No 6113 with superheated boiler at Colwick shed. *T. G. Hepburn*

Bottom: LNER Class B5 No 5185 superheated "Fish Engine" on train of ancient six-wheeled stock at Cleethorpes. *T. G. Hepburn*

Above: GCR 4–6–0 No 1097 *Immingham* with 6ft 7in driving wheels passing Rothley on down express. *L&GRP 16225*

Below: GCR 4–6–0 No 196 with 6ft 9in driving wheels as built. *Locomotive Publishing Co.*

Bottom: Two "Immingham" class 4–6–0s Nos 6100 and 6098, LNER Class B4, at Firsby South Junction on a Leeds–Skegness Saturday train in 1946. *T. G. Hepburn*

Top: GCR 4–6–0 No 425 *City of Manchester. The Rixon Bucknall Collection*.

Above: GCR 4–6–0 No 428 *City of Liverpool* passing Rothley with an up Manchester express. *L&GRP 16216*

Top: LNER Class B2 No 425 *City of Manchester* on the Kings Cross–
Manchester Pullman passing Nottingham Victoria. *T. G. Hepburn*

Above: LNER Class B2 No 5427 *City of London*, in final LNER green livery,
passing Birstall on a down express in 1931. *A. W. Flowers*

Top: GCR mixed traffic 4–6–0 No 443 fitted for oil burning. *The Rixon Bucknall Collection*

Centre: LNER Class B8 No 4 *Glenalmond* in early LNER livery with L&NER on tender, while retaining GCR number and plate, on stopping train at Nottingham Victoria. *T. G. Hepburn*

Above: LNER Class B8 No 5280 with "flower pot" chimney picking up stock for stopping train to Leicester from centre road at Nottingham Victoria in 1929. *A. W. Flowers*

exists. They became LNER Class B5.

The rebuilding of a "Fish Engine" was planned just before the grouping but not carried out until 1923, when No 184 appeared with a superheated boiler pitched high with considerable daylight showing between boiler and frames. This high pitching was needed to allow the larger firebox to clear the rear axle. It was no longer considered economic policy to build non-standard boilers for a class of 14 engines. A rather short, side-windowed cab was fitted to No 184 and this proved inconvenient in that the driver was in danger of damaging his knuckles when turning the reversing screw. The firing was also inconvenient due to the raised cab. The engine retained its slide valves, but a Leicester crew who worked it on a Skegness excursion soon after rebuilding formed a good impression of an engine well on top of its work. Further rebuildings kept the normal cab.

A photograph, taken by the late H. L. Salmon, has been published showing a superheated "Fish Engine" leaving Pertrrborough on an excursion train from the Lincolnshire coast to Kings Cross, consisting of a really dreadful rake of four-wheeled close-coupled suburban stock dating back to the mid-Stirling era. In the 1920s, an engine of this class often worked the train from Lincoln to Grantham connecting with the up "Mark Lane", 8.30 from Grantham. It returned to Lincoln on the stopping train and then worked the York portion of the "North Country Continental", returning with the evening train and sometimes ending its day with another trip to Grantham. In later years "Imminghams" or "Sir Sam Fays" were on this job.

Following his 0–8–0s and 4–6–0s, Robinson took the big engine policy a step further in 1903/4 when he ordered from Beyer Peacock and Co four experimental engines, two Atlantics and two 4–6–0s:

Loco No	GC Class	Class LNER	Cylinders	Firebox H.S.	Colour
192	8B	C4	19½×26	153 sq ft	Green
194	8B	C4	19 ×26	153 ,, ,,	Green
195	8C	B1 (B18)	19½×26	140 ,, ,,	Green
196	8C	B1 (B18)	19 ×26	140 ,, ,,	Black

Robinson might well have been influenced by the GWR, where Swindon was building both Atlantics and 4–6–0s for the same work, but Swindon finally decided that the 4–6–0 was the type to be multiplied, where as the GCR opted for the Atlantic. The subsequent history of the GCR could encourage the belief that a good 4–4–0 proved better than either, but the Atlantics had their supporters among enginemen right to the end. The Atlantics and 4–6–0s were intended for easy conversion, but in the event the 4–6–0s finished their lives as six-coupled engines.

The four experimental locomotives had minor variations as well as being of two different wheel arrangements. The six-coupled engines had slightly smaller fireboxes in order to clear the rear coupled axles, but the grate area of 26sq ft was the same. There was more difficulty in locating an ash-pan of adequate size on the 4–6–0.

The four engines had balanced slide valves and Stephenson Link motion and at first they had piston tail rods. They had the standard tenders holding 3250 gallons of water and five tons of coal. The choice of black paint for No 196 was remarked on by The Rev W. J. Scott in 1905, when he described a very fast run with a light load of four bogies or 120 tons: the 23·4 miles from Nottingham to Leicester were run in 23min 42sec and the 103·1 miles from Leicester to Marylebone in 101min 54sec—fast work for an engine in goods livery. C. Rous Marten was timing No 196 at about the same period and he recorded a run of 22min 29sec from Nottingham to Leicester, but 64 seconds longer than his clerical friend from Leicester up to Marylebone. He added that no single-wheeler could have run the train more easily. In 1905 there was still a strong school of thought that looked askance at six-coupled wheels for high speed. Neither No 195 nor No 196 ever proved Rous Marten's claim that the run could have been made with double or treble the load, but other 4–6–0s of little greater size and weight did so. No 196 had a spell working into Grantham from Retford and it was a point of honour for the GCR men to show that their engine could hold its own with the best that the GNR could offer. While both designs were in their saturated flat valve state No 196 displayed at least an edge over the GN Atlantics.

In 1906 ten more 4–6–0s of almost exactly the same design were built by Beyer Peacock and Co. For some reason the driving wheels were two inches less in diameter, ostensibly to improve the uphill work of the engines but possibly for a more sensible practical reason. The Atlantics meanwhile had established a numerical superiority, but the new 4–6–0 shared a good deal of the top link work, though in rather a desultory fashion. They never matched the long run of the Atlantics on top link duties from Leicester shed. The down "Mail", leaving Marylebone at 10pm, was worked regularly by No 195, but when not available an "Immingham" took its place. The new series gained this title after No 1097 had been named *Immingham* when it was chosen to run a Directors' Special to Grimsby in August, 1906 in connection with the work on the new docks.

On August 8, 1908, No 1102 worked a special through from Marylebone to Grimsby via High Wycombe, Bagthorpe Junction and Gainsborough. Driver J. Stewart was in charge throughout. In 1908 No 1100 took a Grand National Race special from Clee-thorpes with a load of 22 coaches, presumably six-wheelers. On

Sunday April 26, 1914 an Atlantic had stalled at Canfield Place owing to slipping in the tunnels and "Immingham" No 1096 was sent to give rear end assistance, but unfortunately struck the rear too hard with considerable damage and injuries to 17 passangers. For a short time No 6097 (LNER numbering) was allocated to Leicester and although the engine still had slide valves, Driver Fowler worked it on a number of top link expresses with no trouble; these included the northbound Newspaper to Sheffield, with its 22min booking to Arkwright Street, Nottingham, and the return 7.30 from Sheffield.

At first the "Imminghams" were green, then they were repainted in the goods black, all being dealt with by mid-1908. In LNER days they were green before reverting to black in wartime. When superheated they were given 21in cylinders and 10in piston valves, while the cramped ashpan was modified. In this form they did some good work, especially over the GNR main line. Success depended on correct firing; this involved getting used to the shallow firebox and firing without hitting the brick arch and putting it all in the middle. It was a question of keeping the right arm up and tipping the shovel at an angle by which the coal took a downward path into the box. When the GNR men mastered the technique good results followed. The "Imminghams" became LNER Class B4.

Two months after the "Immingham" order, Beyer Peacock delivered ten similar goods 4-6-os. These had 19¼in cylinders and 5ft 3in driving wheels. They had, perhaps, more in common with the "Fish Engines" in that the grate area was 23·4sq ft, though otherwise the boiler was similar to that of the "Imminghams". With brass beading round the splashers these engines looked attractive in the GCR black if well cleaned. They were intended to take over some of the harder and faster duties then given to the o-6-o "Pom-Poms" and were mainly on goods work, but at times had to take a share in passenger working.

From 1906 to the 1920s almost the whole class was shared between Gorton, Lincoln and Grimsby; the Lincoln engines took forward fruit trains from the GER. There was one loner, No 1114, booked as being a Mexborough engine but shedded at Bradford GN; it worked a nightly fast goods from Bradford to Manchester. Photographs exist of these engines working troop specials during army manoeuvres in 1910 and of one leaving Leicester with one of the cross-country expresses from the GWR. Superheating and 21in cylinders put new life into the class, though their appearance was thereafter less attractive with the excessive daylight under the boiler. The whole class ended its days at Trafford Park and Gorton.

In retrospect it would appear that the path to a really good GCR 4-6-o lay ahead if the simple 4-6-o with two outside cylinders had been further developed, but 4-6-o design took a different turn into what proved to be something of a blind alley. The next Gorton 4–6–0 appeared in 1912 when six large inside-cylinder express engines were built.

It is difficult to see the reason for adopting this arrangement for so massive a machine. The only British precedent for so large a 4–6–0 with inside cylinders was the Caledonian *Cardean* class. These had a considerable reputation among amateur critics of engine looks, but their general everyday work was not equal, size for size, to that of the Caledonian 4–4–0s. It is true that there had been an impressive output of maximum hp by No 903 *Cardean* on the climb from Carlisle to Shap during trials over the LNWR, but in 1912 no results had been made public. It is possible that the Caledonian people might have revealed something to Gorton during private exchanges, but in those days railway engineers more frequently kept their own council. Whatever the reason, Gorton built some inside-cylinder 4–6–0s even bigger than the "Cardeans".

The inside cylinders were 21½in in diameter, fed by 10in piston valves with inside admission. The boiler was large and gave every impression of power, but it was not well proportioned in that the same 26sq ft grate was relatively small, while the impressive total heating surface area was made up mainly by the tubes. The total heating surface, on paper, was greater than that of Britain's largest 4–6–0, the GWR "King", which had a 34sq ft grate. A contemporary 4–6–0 was the LNWR "Claughton", which had a 30ft grate in a smaller boiler. The "Claughtons" far surpassed the GCR engines in maximum power output. At a later date the GCR built their 4–4–0 "Director" class with the same firebox but a shorter boiler and these engines could produce equal or superior power outputs. The conclusion that suggests itself is that the front end of the long tubes did little real heating. These engines were superheated from the start. It has been argued that the short connecting rods, used when an engine drove on to the leading axle, caused undesirable thrusts on the slide bars, but it is possible to quote examples which caused no trouble.

The first engine, No 423, was named *Sir Sam Fay* after the progressive General Manager knighted by King George V at Immingham Docks during the same year.

Sir Sam Fay was intended to be put on exhibition in Amsterdam and for this it was given a burnished chimney top and the long splashers were finished in claret, but many think the type looked better with green splashers in LNER days. However, the engine could not be spared for exhibition abroad and a model was sent instead.

No 423 had trials on the Chapletown branch with gradients of 1 in 40 and loads of up to 400 tons. There was some trouble with the driving axlebox bearings and for a time the class was restricted to fast freights and semi-fast passenger trains, though during World War I they were frequently used on ambulance and troop trains. The axlebox trouble was eventually remedied and thereafter they worked on the main line expresses between Manchester and Marylebone. A number of impressive photographs were taken of them during this period between the end of hostilities and the grouping of the railways in 1923, but the four-coupled classes still dominated.

Five more of the type, GCR Class I, were built in 1913; two were finished in passenger green but the remaining three were painted goods engine black. In June, 1913 they were named after cities served by the GCR. After grouping some received cylinders lined up to 20in and the heating surface modified by a reduction of the number of tubes, following experience with the four-cylinder 4–6–0s. They spent most of their time north of Leicester, a good deal of it on the route of the old M.S&L.

Cecil J. Allen once tabulated a "Sir Sam Fay" and an Atlantic in parallel columns working the 109min booking from Leicester to Marylebone. The Atlantic was throughout stronger on the banks than the larger 4–6–0s and this pattern of performance was general. In 1937 No 5427 *City of London* lost its nameplate when the streamlined B17, built for the "East Anglian", took the same name. The "Sir Sam Fays", which retained their 21½in cylinders, became LNER Class B2/1 and those with cylinders lined up to 20in, Class B2/2. They were painted green in LNER days, but became black during World War II. When the Thompson two-cylinder rebuild of Class B17 was introduced in 1945 the former GCR B2s were reclassified B19, finally becoming extinct in November, 1947.

Before the last of the "Sir Sam Fays" took the road the first of a mixed traffic version of the same engine emerged, with 5ft 7in driving wheels and the same boiler and long continuous splashers. The first was No 4, *Glenalmond*, named after the Scottish home of the Chairman of the company. If the "Sir Sam Fays" are considered as the Great Central counterparts of the Caledonian "Cardeans", then the "Glenalmonds" were the equivalent of the McIntosh 908 Class, except that the Caledonian mixed traffic engines had shorter boilers than the express engines (incidentally, one of the McIntosh 908s was named *Barochan* after the residence of the Caledonian Chairman). There is no real evidence that the McIntosh engines were the inspiration of Robinson's inside cylinder 4–6–0s, but the Scottish designer and his engines had a high reputation at that time.

The "Glenalmonds" were classified 1A and worked express freight and secondary passenger trains with a few appearances on expresses. They became LNER Class B8 and remained in black throughout their lives. Some had their cylinders lined up to 20in, but others retained 21½in cylinders to the end. Those with the larger cylinders were LNER Class B8/1 and those lined up B8/2. The last engine was withdrawn in April, 1949, still with the larger cylinders.

World War I put a stop to new construction, but design work must have proceded in the drawing office for two prototype 4-6-os appeared towards the end of the war. During the 1914-18 war locomotive building had to be limited and such engines as were built were designated goods or mixed traffic. So it was that on December 13, 1917 a mysterious note appeared in the GCR Locomotive Committee Minute Book to the effect that "somewhat of an experimental engine had been building during the past two years as opportunity permitted". This was described as a four-cylinder mixed traffic locomotive, but it emerged as No 1169 *Lord Faringdon*. Perhaps it was necessary to describe No 1169 as "mixed traffic" to avoid a Government standstill just as the "Merchant Navy" class Pacifics on the SR could only be built if they were labelled "mixed traffic". But it might also be that No 1169 was regarded as an experimental modification to the "Sir Sam Fays", which were not considered to be fully established express engines, as three of the class were painted black.

Completed in November, 1917 No 1169 *Lord Faringdon*, Class 9P, was the first four-cylinder 4-6-0 on the GCR. It was an engine of most impressive appearance, combining a modified "Sir Sam Fay" class boiler with four cylinders, which suggests that the weaknesses of the inside-cylinder 4-6-os had been recognised. It has been said that the GCR "Director" class 4-4-os had been inspired by the success of the LNWR "George the Fifth" 4-4-os of about the same size and weight; if that were so then the "Lord Faringdons" were the GCR "Claughtons". The boiler was externally the same as that of a "Sir Sam Fay", but there was a rearrangement of the tubes. It has been suggested by critics that the 26sq ft of grate area was insufficient for so large an engine. The GWR "Stars" and "Saints" were, however, showing their ability to sustain 1500–1600ihp with short bursts at 1700–1800hp from a 27sq ft grate. If the boiler had been correctly proportioned 1400–1600ihp should have been possible with a 26sq ft grate. The "Lord Faringdons" were beautifully built and finished, and their impressive appearance raised the hopes of GCR enthusiasts.

The advantages hoped for from the use of four cylinders were a reduction of stresses and better balancing; the disadvantages were greater complication and inaccessibility of the inside motion. Some designers went to considerable lengths to obtain connecting rods of equal length on all four sets of motion. Churchward secured it by setting the inside cylinders forward to drive the leading axle while the outside cylinders, set back level with the rear bogie axle, drove the middle pair of driving wheels. On the LNWR Bowen Cooke set his cylinders in line and all four drove the leading axle. Robinson, on the GCR, tried to combine some of the best features of each method by having his cylinders in line but retaining divided drive. To keep the difference in length between inside and outside rods to a minimum he used very long outside piston rods with the cross heads supported by guides set well back from the cylinders. He was thus able to use standard outside connecting rods which, although longer than the inside rods, were shorter and lighter than they would otherwise have been.

The four 16in × 26in cylinders were fed by 8in piston valves worked by Stephenson Link motion with eccentrics on the leading coupled axle; a rocking shaft extended through the frames to activate the outside valves. The inside cyli..ders had inside admission and the outside valves had outside admission. The whole arrangement was a compromise which avoided the complication of four sets of gear, but it did not give the almost perfect balancing expected of a four-cylinder engine. The "Lord Faringdons" were, however, good riding engines, thanks partly to four cylinders but partly to the solidity of Robinson's designs. This good riding was remembered by men who in LNER and BR days had to work classes of 4-6-0 which, although superior in thermal efficiency, were notorious for the rough ride they gave their crews. Many a GCR man, shaken up on a B17 or a B1, looked back to his days on Robinson's 4-6-0s and was ready to forgive their heavy coal consumption.

Five more "Lord Faringdons" were built in 1920, four carrying names associated with the 1914-1918 war. No 1165 was the GCR War Memorial and carried the name *Valour* and a suitably inscribed plate. The Royal Navy was represented by No 1164 *Earl Beatty* and the Army by No 1166 *Earl Haig*. The wartime Prime Minister *Lloyd George*, had short-lived honour on engine No 1167; in 1923 the nameplates were removed with his political eclipse, never to be restored. The final engine No 1168 was named *Lord Stuart of Wortley* after a GCR Director. On Remembrance Days in GCR times *Valour* used to haul the 8.20 up, the train stopped at Leicester at 10.58am, and, with a wreath of Flanders poppies on *Valour's* smokebox, the two minutes silence would be observed at the Leicester platform. In later years *Valour* was the centre of a short service held at Gorton. *Valour* had a side-window cab, as did Nos 1166 and 1168.

The LNER made a sustained effort to use these engines to advantage and gave them a spell on the GNR section working the Pullmans, but they yielded to the GN Atlantics. They became LNER Class B3, which was subdivided as modifications were introduced. Those which retained Stephenson Link motion were Class B3/1; B3/2 had Caprotti valve gear; and Class B3/3 was engine No 6166 after drastic rebuilding by Thompson with two outside cylinders and Walschaerts gear in 1943. The class became extinct in December, 1947 except for No 6166, which was almost a replacement, and was withdrawn as No 61497 in April, 1949. Some of the best work of the class was performed from Immingham shed.

The other two experimental engines of 1917 were a large-boilered 2–8–0 and a mixed traffic 4–6–0. This last engine appeared on July 27, 1917 as No 416. The 4–6–0 used the same boiler as the 2–8–0 and it was claimed that 68 per cent of the working parts of both engines were interchangeable. The reversion to two outside cylinders for a mixed traffic 4–6–0 was logical and reasonable and it is difficult to understand why this design was not developed and standardised.

The experimental No 416 was classed 8N by the GCR. Its boiler was not the same as that used on the "Sir Sam Fays", but that of the standard 2–8–0 fattened though not lengthened. Externally the boiler looked much like that of a "Sir Sam Fay", but the barrel was shorter and the smokebox longer. The fact that cylinders and motion were the same on the standard 2–8–0s was, in itself, a good reason for developing the design further. The 2–8–0 was later given the standard boiler, which suggests that the larger boiler was of limited value, but the general reputation of the 4–6–0 was good.

After completion of trials at Gorton No 416 was sent to Neasden and for a couple of years put to work in the "Pipe Train Link"— the fast, fully fitted freights between London and Manchester and London and Grimsby. It was in the hands of Driver Wilson, supported by Fireman Moore, who later went to Kings Cross and there became, eventually, a star man in the post-nationalisation "Elizabethan" Link.

In 1921 two more, Nos 52 and 53, were added to stock; these had a rather cramped side-window cab. They often worked excursions or duplicates to main-line expresses. On fast work they gave less trouble than the inside-cylinder "Glenalmonds", as more reliance could be placed on the outside big ends.

Nos 52 and 53 were sent initially to Woodford, where they put in a good deal of work on the cross-country expresses handed over at Banbury, and went to Gorton in 1922. During the 1925–28 period they worked from Neepsend and were then posted to Ardsley, returning in 1934. At times they worked on the train due in Leicester at 10.58am, returning on the 10am from Marylebone with a schedule of 24min from Leicester to Nottingham and 48min on to Sheffield; we have heard that they could maintain this timing but no reliable logs exist. It is reported that No 5416 had to take over a Cup Final Special when the specially prepared B17 No 2849 *Sheffield United* failed, but some accounts say that a "Glenalmond" was involved. This is a natural point of confusion since all three engines were frequently grouped as "outside cylinder Glenalmonds" by the men, but the preponderance of evidence suggests that it really was No 5416. These engines were LNER Class B6 and they became extinct in December, 1947. In view of the logical simplicity of this design and the high regard with which the three engines are still spoken of by retired former GCR enginemen, it is strange that no more than three were built.

The last of the long line of GCR 4–6–os entered service in 1921, when the first of the GCR Class 9Q appeared. These were mixed traffic versions of the "Lord Faringdons", with the same boiler, cylinders and motion as the express engines. It may be questioned if there was much wisdom in accepting the complication of four cylinders for mixed traffic engines, but evidently Gorton had decided that this policy was correct—certainly they had experimented enough with the various two-cylinder classes. With hindsight it might be concluded that more attention to improving small details would have been more sensible than building more and building bigger. The Class 9Q mixed traffic engines became the most numerous class of 4–6–o on the GCR, reaching a total of 28 engines. Ten more were added by the LNER.

The various ideas tried out by the GCR came to culmination with these locomotives. Top feed, which had been tried earlier, was fitted to the 9Qs, a difference as compared with the "Lord Faringdons". The express engines had both plain and side-window cabs, but the side-window cab now became standard on the mixed traffic engines.

The GCR locomotives were built mainly at Gorton, but ten came from the Vulcan Foundry and five from Beyer Peacock. The further ten built after the grouping all emerged from Gorton in 1923/4. These LNER engines were built with reduced boiler mountings so that they fitted the general loading gauge. Most of the class remained on the GCR, but they sometimes penetrated the NE section on specials, while the Immingham engines at times ran up to Kings Cross on excursions. They were well known at Banbury on the cross-country trains from the GCR.

The smaller driving wheels gave more space between the firebars and the rear axle, which suggested that a bigger and better ashpan was possible. The class had a general reputation for heavy coal consumption, hence their widespread nickname of "Black Pigs". As on many classes, however, coal consumption could be reduced by skilled handling from experienced men who knew the way to produce the best results. They ran up from Manchester to Wembley

on specials to the British Empire Exhibitions of 1924/5 and on Cup
Final trains; had they been as extravagant as legend maintains
the coal would never have lasted the Manchester–London journey.
Many firemen preferred a smooth ride on a "Black Pig" to a rough
ride on a K3, even if the GCR engine did shift some coal. The
reputation of the GCR 9Qs was similar to that of the NER S3s;
both classes were powerful machines, reached similar maximum
speeds and had healthy appetites for coal. Neither was popular
with enginemen from the other railways, but it is possible to find
some of their own men willing to give them a good word.

The LNER made a number of variations to all GCR engines.
The final batch of four-cylinder mixed traffic engines, Nos 5480–4,
had larger steam chests with more widely spaced heads and
strengthened steam passages. Engine No 5480, still in shop grey,
had a short spell at Leicester working the night goods to Manchester.
It was fitted with compression valves on the cylinder ends, which
meant that experiments in the use of solid piston valves in place of the
Robinson pressure release design were taking place. Later, of
course, solid, ring-controlled, piston valves were standardised. On
the LMS the narrow ring valves, by reducing leakage, had a
beneficial effect on coal consumption which was reflected in test
results. On the LNER results are less clearly defined and many
former NER and GCR enginemen still maintain that their engines
were spoilt by LNER "improvements". The Robinson type of
anti-vacuum or snifting valves were replaced, in due course, by
the standard Gresley type behind the chimney. Those 9Qs which
were built in GCR times and which retained their full height were
classified B7/1, while those with reduced mountings and a height
limited to 13ft were Class B7/2. Three of the B7s were fitted with
modified Knorr piston valves in 1927/8. They are well spoken of
by retired enginemen, but the experiment was carried no further.

Of all the external features of a steam locomotive the chimney was
the one which gave the engine character. The Robinson-type
GCR chimney was shapely and it looked very handsome on some
of the 4–6–0s, but in LNER days from 1924 onwards the un-
speakable "flower pot" made its appearance. This aroused great
anger among GCR enthusiasts, who thought that their railway
was the victim of malice. In support they also cited the fact that
the GCR "Atlantics" and "Directors", which regularly hauled
some of the fastest trains on the system, were painted black while
other Atlantics, such as the NER Class Vs and the LNER D49
4–4–0s, which were generally on secondary duties, were turned
out in green. The GCR 4–6–0s spoilt any such theory, because all
those with the larger wheel diameters were painted green regardless
of the fact that they had sunk lower in the social scale. So it was
that the excursion train with its green "Sir Sam Fay" might

be side-tracked for the passage of an express with a black Atlantic or "Director". In the mid-1930s the dreadful flower pots were replaced by a new more shapely chimney, which was a shortened version of the Robinson pattern.

A number of B7s were stationed at Neasden in early LNER days. Some were needed to work the Wembley Exhibition specials and to cover the failures of visiting engines, for many "foreigners" penetrated the GCR during 1924/5. The end of the exhibition and the re-routing of Grimsby fish trains via Boston and Peterborough in the charge of K3s robbed Neasden of its need for so many mixed traffic engines. The B7s did a lot of fast work at holiday times on the cross-country services. They gave little trouble from overheated bearings, but at times they were handicapped by hot big ends, several coming to grief from this malady at the foot of the descent past Whetstone. The nuisance was lessened as Woodford men developed a technique of keeping a breath of steam on when running downhill. Drivers who kept the regulator open and notched up as far as possible limited the demands on the firemen. In the 1940s there were instances of cracked frames; one B7, No 5463 (1371), had to have entirely new frames and others had extension pieces welded on in front of the smokebox No. 1371 ran for a time with an O4 chimney.

The Great Central certainly provided much variety for the enthusiast, but the economist must deplore the building of nine classes of 4-6-0 when one, or two at the most, would have sufficed. Among the ranks of the GCR 4-6-0s were some very good-looking and very interesting locomotives. At times they did some good work, but it must be recorded that no GCR 4-6-0 ever showed a significant improvement over the Atlantics or the "Directors".

CHAPTER FIVE

The Performance of the Pre-Grouping 4-6-0s

The LNER was not a wealthy railway and vast capital expenditure on new locomotives was not possible. This meant that the older locomotives of the constituent companies had to carry a heavy burden for longer than was really desirable. There was a good side to this in that there was less resentment among LNER men at the replacement of familiar locomotives than on the LMS following "Midlandisation". Some discontent was voiced on the LNER over the transfer of alien designs to railways where loyalties were strong, but it was never on the scale of the storm which followed the introduction of Midland compounds on the Euston–Birmingham services in place of the "Georges". Among the older types of locomotive which had to carry on in service right up to the end of the LNER's independent existence were a number of 4–6–0 classes. In some cases the tasks allotted to them were accomplished only by the highest traditions of enginemanship.

By the time the North Eastern became part of the LNER the 4–6–0 had been outclassed by the Atlantic for the fastest main line expresses, but the railways in the 1920s carried very heavy seasonal traffic, when every available engine had to be called in to move the trains. Under such conditions a fleet of mixed traffic 4–6–0s was a great asset to the NER. In 1924 Cecil J. Allen had a surprisingly brisk run from Darlington to York behind S2 class 4–6–0 No 798 with a load of 300 tons tare or 350 tons gross. At first the run proceeded as might be expected, with speeds nowhere higher than 66mph; then, after Northallerton the engine made a spurt for home, rising finally to 74mph at Alne and maintaining 68mph to Benningborough. This was far above the usual speeds of up to 65mph which were normally the maximum for this class. The maximum of 74mph down a grade of 1 in 805 was, up till then, the fastest that this very experienced recorder had recorded with wheels of 6ft 1in diameter. Even the 6ft 3in 4–6–0 "Princes" of the LNWR had needed a little more assistance from gravity to reach speeds in the 70s. It would have needed a rather strong faith, however, to have claimed that an S2 could have been entrusted every day with a 3½ hour Manchester or Liverpool express from Euston with a 350 ton load as was habitual with the "Princes".

A few years later one of the larger S3 (LNER B16) class three-cylinder 4–6–0s, No 1382, was at the head of a 13-coach train of

427 tons, tare, 450 tons full, over the same course. Despite its 5ft 8in driving wheels the engine made a very slow start. The idea that small wheels automatically ensured quick starting has little support in recorded performance, because this same tendency towards moderate starts was also shared, frequently, by the GCR B7s and the GNR K3s. After passing Northallerton, however, matters improved and speed rose to 66½mph at Alne. Signal delays made the time to the stop at York 50min 49sec, but the net time was 48min against 45¾min by the two-cylinder B15 with a load 100 tons less. The Darlington–York road was especially suited to fast finishes; the engine either coming off at York or the train was making a long stop, during which the boiler could recover pressure and water level.

Another B16, No 2369, was called upon to take the place of a 4-4-0 "Shire" class engine on one of the smartly timed Leeds–York trains. The load was 205 tons tare, 210 tons full, and an unchecked entry into York would have made the start-to-stop time 29min for the 25·5 miles. The maximum speed down Mickefield Bank was 77mph. This compares in interesting fashion with the fastest speeds recorded with the GCR B7 class 4-6-0s, also with 5ft 8in driving wheels. The B16s were useful substitutes for express engines on all but the fastest bookings. They did considerable work on summer Saturdays on specials to Bridlington or Scarborough and as many as 30 could be seen in Scarborough locomotive yard on August Saturday afternoons.

The North Eastern 4-6-0s often visited the Great Central in LNER days and the opinions of "foreign" enginemen are of interest. The original B13s were considered "flat road trudgers", with no liveliness at all. They gave a good ride, with no trouble in maintaining steam, and would rattle and bang, but there were not many failures on the road with overheated bearings. They were of course getting old by the time they visited the GCR, but they were never really suitable for fast goods trains over the GCR grades.

The passenger Class B14 4-6-0s also visited the GCR on the Dringhouses–Woodford–Banbury fast goods. These ran unbraked at Class A speed allowing a heavier load at a lower speed. The B14s had heavy rasping exhausts and burnt a good fire even with some clinker in the box. Despite their large wheels and despite some earlier recorded fast running, they were rather sluggish in their old age. The secret of good steaming was to have a level fire over the whole grate, not too deep under the fire-hole, and to allow plenty of secondary air. The original Smith's patent segmented piston valve had been replaced long before these engines visited the GCR. They worked specials from Leeds to Cleethorpes on occasions.

The B15 class gave little trouble on the Dringhouse trains, as the larger boiler caused less worry about steaming. They were able to climb the banks and could get along well over the easier stretches—in fact, it was possible to gain time with these engines even with full loads. They made plenty of noise from the chimney top. Their tenders were not well designed for the fireman. They had a wedge-shaped front, with the flow of coal depending on two or three thick planks of wood fitting into grooves; these planks were made immovable by the pressure of the coal and large lumps could not get through.

The larger B16s were not favoured, although it was admitted that they were big, powerful machines. The cab was considered to be cramped, the fire hole was not conveniently situated and the longer firebox meant harder work in throwing the coal forward. The two injectors made life easier. Such an engine was not given a banker up Staveley Bank, where the music from the chimney was glorious but hardly appreciated by the fireman, who had little time to listen. The B16s rarely worked Class C fully fitted freights on the GCR, but occasionally they were on the GWR-to-NER vegetable train known as "The Veggies". All the NE section fast goods (Class C) to the Southern Area were rostered for K3 haulage before the building of the V2s, but the goods services to Ardsley, Hull and Whitemoor usually had B16s. Everybody agreed that the B16s rode better than the K3s and the "Big Ravens" were popular with their own NER men, many of whom had little regard for anything GCR. The Gresley and Thompson rebuilds were better engines altogether.

The GER B12s were employed on first-class express duties right up to the end of the LNER's existence. Much of this work in the pre-war period was of a very high standard in relation to the size of the engine. The criterion of GER locomotive performance was the nightly "Continental" from Liverpool Street to Parkeston Quay. The energetic reforms of the American-trained General Manager, Sir Henry Thornton, had introduced Pullman cars on to the GER and two of these were added to the "Hook Continental", which meant that the load was frequently over 400 tons. The schedule has been eased from the pre-war 82min, but after hostilities were over the 82min booking was restored despite the additional load. It had been mentioned in Chapter 3 that initial test runs had shown B12 class engines capable of reaching Parkeston Quay in 75min with 331tons and in 82min with 440 tons, but in the post-war world the test run timing was expected to be kept every night with over 400 tons and a schedule of 82min. Timekeeping under such conditions was a job for the most expert of engine crews only. The hour supplied the men, for in the four top-link crews at Parkeston shed ability was combined with enthusiasm.

The 1 in 70 rise to Bethnal Green was the first obstacle and then, just as the engine was recovering speed, came the 30mph slack through Stratford, after which recovery up gradual rising grades was essential to gain impetus for Brentwood Bank, with its 3·3 miles of 1 in 105 and a short length of 1 in 77. After that the effort could be eased slightly, but the 40mph restrictions through Chelmsford and Colchester prevented any long stretch of high-speed running. Finally, a 20mph slack marked the junction of the Harwich branch with the main Ipswich line at Manningtree. There was no break anywhere and an error in judgement could put the train seriously behind time. The whole situation was redeemed only by the fact that the really hard work was over within twenty miles and the whole journey in well under an hour-and-a-half.

In 1922 Cecil J. Allen rode on the footplate of engine No 1565 on the "Hook Continental" with Driver Chris Osborne and Fireman Knappett. The load was ten corridor bogie coaches, two Pullman cars each of 42 tons and a six-wheeled van, which weighed 388 tons tare and 420 tons with a full complement of passengers. They had a perfectly clear road throughout and with cut off advanced to 40 per cent topped Brentwood Bank at a minimum speed of 32·8 mph. Parkeston Quay was reached in 81min 5sec, almost a minute early.

A few days later Mr Allen joined the same train on No 1566 with Driver Chapman and Fireman Dale. This crew knew what had happened on the previous occasion and were determined that their running would be no less notable. A slightly less crowded train meant that the gross load was slightly less at 415 tons. They were going well just twenty seconds ahead of their rivals when the Brentwood Yard signals were on and refused to fall until the speed had dropped by several mph at the foot of the formidable Brentwood Bank. Chapman advanced his cut off to 50 per cent with full regulator and, with the voice of No 1566 rousing the echoes for miles around, they mounted the upper section of the bank at an unvarying 33mph, still fifteen seconds ahead as they passed Ingrave Box. As they passed Chelmsford in 36½min all previous records in Mr Allen's experience had been broken. After that easier running, with 25 per cent cut off and a reduced regulator opening brought the train into Parkeston Quay in 80min 15sec or in 80min net. No layman's description can fully appreciate the efforts of a skilled crew performing a hard job with a relatively small engine.

At much the same time Cecil J. Allen also rode on the engine of the post-war equivalent of the old "Norfolk Coast Express" with a gross load of 340 tons. The post-war trains had seven minutes more than its predecessor to cover the 130 miles to North Walsham but a number of slacks made the net time almost exactly the old 157min allowance. This run was performed with the greatest of ease on 30 per cent cut off and half regulator and rather less noise on Brentwood Bank. Mr Allen recorded an ample supply of steam, thanks to the skilled work of Fireman Iles, and the careful handling by Driver Matthews contributed to a moderate coal consumption. Most of the work by the B12s was similar to this, well within the capacity of the engine.

In 1924 the relatively light GER corridor stock on the "Continental" was replaced by new LNER standard stock of heavier tare weight and the schedule eased to 87min. Even with a load of 450 tons this was easier work than the old schedule and the B12s continued to work with satisfaction until relieved by the new B17 "Sandringham" class in 1928. The new engines did not justify a return to the old booking. The B12s showed their ability to handle heavy loads when No 8501 (LNER numbering) with a load of 438 tons tare and 470 tons full, 16 bogies of the GER stock, passed Manningtree in 73min 50 sec and reached Ipswich in 87min 5sec against a booking of 90min. Had the train been a "Continental" and turned off at Manningtree it could have reached Parkeston Quay just inside the lengthened schedule. The B12s still demonstrated their capacity for hard work even into the late 1930s, when most of the heavier duties had been taken over by the B17s or by those B12s which had been extensively rebuilt with larger boilers into Class B12/3. Mr Allen timed No 8534, in original condition save for the addition of ACFI feed-water heating equipment, on an Ipswich express with a load of 383 tons tare, 400 tons full, when Ipswich was reached in a net time of 76½min for the 68·7 miles, which would have meant an arrival at Parkeston Quay just inside the old 82min booking.

The engines with Lentz poppet valves had a reputation for being faster than the standard B12s, but were considered less strong on the banks, though there is little real evidence in published recordings. The original B12s reached speeds of up to or just over 85mph on the GER. There is a record of No 8551 with five bogies of 162 tons tare, 170 tons gross reaching 86mph through Wickford on the Southend branch, but a performance of greater merit in view of the load was that of No 8562 with a 9 coach train of 295 tons tare, 310 tons gross which was worked from Stowmarket to Norwich, 34·4 miles, in 35min 30sec or in 35min net. The train passed mp 112 in 30min 30sec from the Stowmarket start and reached 85mph before Diss.

A most exacting task set to B12 class engines was the through working of the "North Country Continental" from Ipswich to Manchester, a distance of 220 miles with a heavy train over easy grades on the GN and GE Joint Line, but with heavy grades to face between Sheffield and Manchester when the fire might have been expected to be in poor condition. The climb to Woodhead needed full boiler pressure. The load was frequently 14 bogies at the Ipswich end but 5–8 bogies over the Pennines.

In 1924 two B12s turned up at Leicester GC with specials for the Wembley Exhibition; these had 11 bogies each and Stratford drivers. GCR men were provided as pilot-men and they were favourably impressed by the way the GER engines climbed the 1 in 176 banks through Ashby and towards Catesby Tunnel. No trouble was experienced though the GER engines needed to be extended. The timings of these specials would, of course, be easier than the GCR expresses.

Some of the Lentz poppet valve engines were temporarily allocated to Gorton shed before moving to the GER, but it was soon discovered that they were weak on the banks. Downhill they could run as fast as the road permitted. They were troublesome at starting compared with the piston valve engines. As far as the published record goes the difference is less sensational, No 8577 climbed Brentwood Bank with 425 tons at a minimum of 28mph as against Driver Chapman's 33mph with 415 tons on a piston valve engine. There is nothing reliably recorded by a Lentz-valve engine as fast as 85–86mph, but these maxima were attained in later years after the poppet-valve engines were converted to piston valves and when general standards of fast running were higher, partly due to the values set by the rebuilt B12/3s. The experience of the GER section poppet-valve engines, in general, was similar to the results obtained elsewhere. The more complete rebuilding into Class B12/3 is dealt with in another chapter.

The Great Central was a railway of character; what it lacked in riches it made up for in pride. Although it gained its greatest share of honours, by the efforts of its four-coupled locomotives, the "Directors" and Atlantics, the work of its 4–6–0s was not quite as trivial as has been suggested. If the record is fairly examined it will be found that there is some honour due to the locomotives and much honour due to the men.

The two original express passenger 4–6–0s, Nos 195/6 on the GCR, became Nos 5195/6 on the LNER. In GCR days they had done some good work both on their own line and on the GNR. No 195 for many years had worked the 10pm down Mail, having its own regular crew, Driver J. Stevens and Fireman C. Watkins, and during World War I this train was often very heavy, filling most of the long platform at Leicester. No 196 had disturbed the complacency of the more self-satisfied GNR people by the way in which it covered the ground between Grantham and Retford. When 195 was in the shed "Immingham" class B4 4–6–0s deputised on the down Mail. The "Imminghams" had worked most of the GCR expresses; at one time or another the whole class had worked from Neasden. In LNER days the main duties of the B1 and B4 classes was on secondary work, such as the cheap trip specials on

Sundays and the Immingham Boat specials. Such work was not to be despised and they were occasionally called out to haul relief portions to the main line expresses.

A number of B4s, Nos 1095/6/8, 1100/1/2/3/4, were allocated to Neepsend and from there they worked the Bradford–Marylebone expresses to Leicester and also trains to Manchester, Liverpool, Cleethorpes, Hull etc. At that time none had superheaters and all were fitted with slide valves. When a number of Ivatt large Atlantics were sent to Neepsend after the grouping the B4s were switched to March, Doncaster and Ardsley. On the inside of each cab was a board carrying the insciption: "This engine must not work south of March". It was not clever to have sent some so near to temptation, but the intention was most likely to use them only on the GN & GE Joint line to Doncaster, York and Leeds. In due course they received superheaters and their work on the GNR section was at times very good.

The "Imminghams" were used a lot between Leeds and Doncaster, handing over their trains to Pacifics which, until Calder Bridge was strengthened, were not allowed between Doncaster and Leeds. On some turns they worked through to Grantham and occasionally on excursion trains up to Kings Cross. On the Grantham workings some good running was recorded by R. N. Clements. On the best run, with a load of 427 tons tare, 450 tons gross, No 6104 ran the 17·4 miles from Doncaster to Retford in 20min 55sec start to stop and followed this with 33·1 miles from Retford to Grantham in 39min 30sec. This work was comparable with the best normal work of the Ivatt Atlantics, though these engines occasionally rose to exceptional prodigies of effort when taking the place of Pacifics on loads of 500 tons or over. On another run the B4 class engine No 6095 with a load of 370 tons, tare, 390 tons gross, ran from Doncaster to Retford in 20min 30sec, with speed rising on level track from 65 at Ranskill to 67 at Barnby Moor. The Retford–Grantham run took 38min 5sec, with a maximum of 70mph at Crow Park and a minimum of 50mph at Peascliffe.

The gradients are steeper between Leeds and Doncaster, but the late R. E. L. Charlewood, a most careful recorder of vast experience, timed No 6096 with a load of 287 tons tare, 305 tons full, to cover the 9·4 miles from Holbeck to Wakefield in a net start-to-stop time of 14min 40sec. This included a start up 1 in 50 and 3 miles of 1 in 100. At Wakefield more coaches were added, bringing up the load to 14 bogies weighing 438 tons tare and 465 tons full. On this section the grades are a little less severe, but the rise to Nostell Summit includes 3½ miles at 1 in 150. The 19·9 miles from Wakefield to Doncaster were run in 22min 52sec, with a signal check outside Wakefield, or in 22min 22sec net. The uphill work of the "Immingham" class in this area was similar in merit to the everyday work of the GER unrebuilt B12s on their own road.

During World War II a heavily-loaded train ran from Newcastle to Ashford via the GCR, Banbury and Reading. In the later stages of hostilities it loaded to fantastic tonnages, up to 21 bogies having been observed hauled by a V2 with a GNR Atlantic as pilot. Earlier it was more usually 14-15 bogies and on this the timing of 29min from Leicester to Rugby was easily kept by a good V2. On one occasion a former GCR 4–6–0, No 5196—the engine which, in its earlier non-superheated days, used to streak across the Trent Valley at 80mph in competition with the GNR Atlantics—had to tackle a load of 14 bogies weighing 490 tons full. The GCR veteran touched 44½mph at Whetstone, fell to 34½mph up the 7 miles of 1 in 176, reached 59 at Lutterworth and fell to 54 on the short rise beyond, finally attaining 70½mph before slowing for the stop at Rugby in 29min 16sec start to stop. This was a good effort for an aging locomotive of moderate dimensions in wartime. It may be claimed, with some justice, that the earlier GCR 4–6–0s with two outside cylinders performed the best work, size for size, of any of the GCR 4–6–0s.

The Class B2 4–6–0s, the "Sir Sam Fays", were bigger and heavier than the "Imminghams" and should have been more powerful on the road. It is doubtful if they ever proved to be. One of the best heavy load performances which can be traced to this class took place on December 20, 1918 when No 423 *Sir Sam Fay* had a train of 428 tons tare, 465 tons gross, into which had been crowded 700 passengers. *Sir Sam Fay* worked this train from Nottingham Vic to Leicester, 23·3 miles, in 28min 11sec start to stop; Loughborough was passed in 17min 7sec from the Nottingham start. This was comparable in merit to the run by the "Immingham" class engine with the same load from Wakefield to Doncaster, but it did not show the superiority which might have been expected from the bigger engine. This "Sir Sam" run was also far more of an exception than the "Immingham" run. The heavy load Nottingham–Leicester run was recorded by R. E. L. Charlewood.

In the field of high speed a run timed by R. N. Clements was above the general standard. This took place on the 11pm, which on Saturday nights was the equivalent of the weekday "Newspaper". The 11pm down was unusual in that it ran through Nottingham without stopping, carrying its full load of Sunday papers to Sheffield. No 5426 *City of Chester* was at the head of a 10-coach train of 325 tons loaded when timed by R. N. Clements. Loughborough was passed at 85mph and the impetus carried the train over Barnston Summit at a minimum of 69mph. After this the engine was eased and the maximum at Gotham was a more ordinary 76mph. Possibly, though not certainly, the engine was slightly winded after its fast start, but after passing Nottingham Vic. in 23min 50sec from the Leicester start, over a minute early, it put out little energy uphill between Nottingham and Sheffield, which was reached 50sec late. Frequently with these engines and their four-cylinder counterparts a short spell of hard work was followed by some more pedestrian running.

Sir Sam Fay was involved in the Loughborough accident of January 1933, and attention was focused on the stopping distance following the sighting of the Loughborough outer distant. Test runs were made to establish the distance required to stop a train travelling at full speed approaching Loughborough, using "Sir Sam Fay" and GN Atlantic type engines on loads of five and eight bogies. The Class B2 engine used was No 5427 *City of London*, which reached 84mph with five bogies and 81mph with eight bogies. The GN Atlantic No 4412 reached 90mph with the lighter train and 84mph with the heavier. The performance of the Atlantic was slightly better, except that the 4-6-0 made a faster initial start from Leicester with the eight-coach train. Another run timed in everyday service by R. N. Clements had a similar start from Leicester and reached 75mph before slowing for the Loughborough stop. It was followed by much less energy on to Nottingham. These runs in LNER days would be made after the cylinders were lined up to 20in diameter and after some re-arrangements of the tubes. After superheating, the "Imminghams" had been given 21in cylinders and 10in piston valves and would, in addition, occasion less worry about overheating as compared with an engine which must have put some strain on its leading axle if pressed to a maximum effort for any long period.

The Class B3 four-cylinder 4-6-0s had the same boiler as the B2 and a similar performance pattern, but at a slightly higher level. They were not as successful as was hoped, but they were not the complete failures which many writers have suggested. Their reputation was not enhanced by their running on the GNR section Pullman car trains in the early days of grouping. There is little doubt that on this service they were inferior to the Ivatt Atlantics, which ran faster and burnt less coal. Had the GCR 4-6-0s been used on GNR trains which required frequent quick accelerations from stops they might have competed more favourably. Their work on the GN Pullmans was not all bad; some figures published by R. A. H. Weight in 1927 showed that on 28 journeys with an average load of 349 tons and an average net time of 204min for the Kings Cross–Leeds run arrivals were early or punctual on 17 occasions, while on those runs which had suffered delays no arrival was more than 5min late. One of the best runs was not recorded in detail, but the 138 miles from passing Retford to Kings Cross were covered in 135min. Contemporary timekeeping figures for

Atlantic class engines in 1927 were no better, but the GN engines rose to greater heights during the 1930s.

A log of a run by a B3 on a Pullman working was published by Cecil J. Allen in 1927; the engine was No 6165 *Valour*, with a load of 300 tons. The running was more notable for high downhill speeds than for strong hill-climbing, as a maximum of 85mph was reached on the descent of Stoke Bank. This was the general pattern of B3 performance, both on the GN and the GC, but it is unsafe to generalise about the steam locomotive. Thus, in the Charlewood note-book there is a run by No 6168 *Lord Stuart of Wortley* hauling eight Pullman cars and a van weighing 330 tons loaded, which was characterised by moderate downhill speeds and good hillclimbing; the time up Stoke Bank from mp 85 to mp 100 was 15min 53sec, quite as good as the average contemporary Atlantic time, and 73 miles from mp 80 to mp 153 were covered in 71min 13sec. This run was made in unfavourable weather with a side gale.

The GCR 4-6-0s were withdrawn from the Pullman workings after a few years, but the "Directors" remained for longer and after the 1932 accelerations the Atlantics had the job to themselves until the strengthening of Calder Bridge allowed Pacifics to take over. The "Sir Sam Fay" class engine No 425 *City of Manchester* had a short spell on the ill-fated "Sheffield Pullman", as it was thought that this GCR 4-6-0 would be stronger on the banks between Nottingham and Sheffield than the GN Atlantics. The GCR engines gained a reputation for burning more coal than the piston-valve Atlantics with 32 element superheaters, which achieved net times as short as 173-176min for the Kings Cross-Leeds run, but the visitors took the honours for their good riding in contrast to the wild antics of the GNR machines.

After their ousting from the Pullmans the GCR 4-6-0s continued to visit Kings Cross on specials. The "Imminghams" came up from Leeds while B2s, B3s and sometimes B7s arrived at the head of Eason's Special from Grimsby. Drivers Croft and Cleaver from Immingham shed knew the road through to Kings Cross and were masters of the art of handling Robinson 4-6-0s. Driver Croft with No 6169 *Lord Faringdon*, at that time thought to be the best of the Immingham allocation, ran up from Peterborough in a net time of 80min with a load of 460 tons, and Hitchin was passed in 46$\frac{1}{4}$min for the 44.5 miles. Cecil J. Allen, writing in 1931, declared that the work was equal to normal contemporary Pacific quality until the slight falling off in speed between Hitchin and Stevenage. The edbhp from the Peterborough start to passing Hitchin was 835 and the ihp approximately 1200. The climb from Hitchin to Stevenage works out at 895edbhp and 1120ihp. If the fireman was tiring a little after working through from Grimsby he had every excuse, for the condition of firebox and tubes would possibly have been giving anxiety. Any engine with long tubes and a relatively small grate would need very careful handling on a long run.

In *Steam in the Blood* (Ian Allan, 1971), R. N. H. Hardy records that in 1943 B3s No 6164 *Earl Beatty* and No 6165 *Valour* were transferred to Copley Hill shed, Leeds. No 6164 was in poor condition, but No 6165, straight from the shops and retaining piston valves, was a very good engine. Mr Hardy once fired on *Valour* for Driver Alf Cartwright when the B3 had been called upon to replace a failed V2 at the head of a wartime load of 540 tons, tare, 565 tons full, from Wakefield to Grantham. It was a comfortable journey with the good-riding engine steaming freely and proving itself master of the wartime schedule despite the very heavy load. Driver Cartwright used full regulator whenever it was needed and the first port downhill. The gear was kept as far linked up as the road allowed. Firing was made easier by the fact that coal had just to be placed inside the door; the blast and the motion of the engine did the rest. There was no need for the wrist work needed to fill the back corners of the wide fireboxes of the Pacifics or V2s. It was not claimed that the B3 was the equal of a good V2, but the smaller engine, at the top of its form, gave a better performance than a large one in poor condition.

On the GCR the B3s did some good work. Shortly after construction the four-cylinder 4-6-0s occasionally had to haul very heavy loads. On December 16, 1918 R. E. Charlewood timed No 1169 *Lord Faringdon*, in the flush of vigorous youth, at the head of the 12·15pm down which had been made up by the addition of extras to 394 tons tare, 440 tons with a packed complement of passengers. The train had frequent stops and short runs which were made in a competent fashion, thus:

High Wycombe–Princes Risborough	328/365 tons	8·4 miles	12min 45sec.
Brackley–Woodford	328/365 tons	9·8 miles	12min 28sec.
Woodford–Rugby	394/440 tons	14·1 miles	16min 24sec.
Rugby–Leicester	394/440 tons	19·9 miles	21min 43sec.
Leicester–Loughborough	394/440 tons	9·9 miles	13min 3sec.
Loughborough–Nottingham Vic.	394/440 tons	13·5 miles	17min 27sec.

Work of this type, involving drawing up at many of the stops, was the chance for a 4-6-0 to show its superiority over an Atlantic or large 4-4-0. The nearly new four-cylinder *Lord Faringdon* did well, especially as in 1918 full speed downhill running had not been restored. The start from Leicester, passing Belgrave, 2·3 miles, in 4min 30sec, was excellent with 440 tons, but that from Loughborough was less vigourous.

In ordinary everyday service, with more moderate loads but at higher speeds, the "Directors" and Atlantics dominated, but there was one GCR section train not normally in the public eye on which the B3s long did most of the work. This was the 2·32am down "Newspaper" from Marylebone to Leicester, which for several years was worked by these engines and a special link of three drivers. The story is told, in dramatic fashion, by "5267" in *Essays in Steam* (Ian Allan 1970), following publication in the *Stephenson Locomotive Society Journal*. The tare load was usually 255 tons, but the eight vans were packed to the roof with newsprint, so the total load could have been 300 tons or over. This had to be worked from Marylebone to Brackley, 59·3 miles, in 67min, Brackley to Rugby, 23·9 miles, in 24min and Rugby to Leicester, 19·9 miles, in 20min. There was not a moment's respite anywhere uphill or down and immaculate time-keeping was just out of reach, but even if a few minutes were frequently booked "against the loco" the train required a high standard of enginemanship.

In 1930 the first two B3s to have poppet valves joined Neasden shed, but the improvement was less than had been hoped. The general picture can best be shown by a small table.

From	To	Distance	Best time	Average time	Type
Marylebone–Brackley		59·3 miles	66¾min	68½min	piston valves
Marylebone–Brackley		59·3 miles	65½min	67¼min	Caprotti
Marylebone–Brackley		59·3 miles	66¼min	—	"Director" D10
Brackley–Rugby		23·9 miles	24min 20sec	25¼min	piston valves
Rugby–Leicester		19·9 miles	19min 40sec	20min 18sec	Caprotti

There were individual runs which showed a gain on schedule over short sections of the run, but usually the price had to be paid later. If, for example, the engine was flogged away from the Brackley start up the 1 in 176 then it had to be eased over the down grades that followed and the overall time was no better. Firing was heavy but the task was made easier by the fact that careful placing was not needed, though the fact that the fire-hole was higher than the shovelling plate was not helpful.

The piston valve engines could reach 85mph and they did so on a number of recorded occasions at Braunston, Whetstone, Ruddington and on the descent to Aylesbury. Exactly the same maximum speed was recorded down Stoke Bank and it appears to be much about the same as the maximum for the "Fays". The Caprotti engines were faster and on them 88mph was recorded at Whetstone both by "5267" and by Norman Harvey. The piston-valve engines had a reputation for very heavy coal consumption and although there is little doubt that they burnt more than they should have done, some accounts are exaggerated. It would be impossible, for example, to have made the through run from Marylebone to Manchester on 95 lb of coal per mile. Tales are told of them running short of coal on the nonstop Pullman from Kings Cross to Harrogate, 199 miles, but they certainly managed the Marylebone–Manchester through run of 206 more heavily graded miles with similar loads. There are reliable figures that suggest that they averaged just over or under 60 lb per mile, but lb/mile figures are of less value than lb/dbhp hr and these figures are missing.

The B3s were used on the cheap fare excursion trains run on Sundays and it was on one of these that Norman Harvey timed No 6167, which was fitted with the steam-operated Caprotti valves, in June, 1938. A speed of 88mph was reached at Whetstone with 360 tons. On his return journey Mr Harvey recorded a smart run by No 6166, with the earlier type of spring-operated valves:

B3/2 No 6166 *Earl Haig* Load 10/240/360 tons.				
0·0	Rugby	00min	00sec	mph
4·7	Braunston	6	32	64
		pws		
11·7	Charwelton	14	05	40
14·1	Woodford	16	40	66
17·1	Culworth	19	20	68
20·7	Helmdon	22	35	66
23·9	Brackley	25	27	66
28·7	Finmere	29	52	70
34·4	Calvert	34	20	80
		slack		
39·1	Quainton Road	39	10	54
45·3	Aylesbury arr.	45	49	
Schedule 49min		Net time 45min.		

While this run was most satisfactory, one on the same train during the same month, July, 1939, timed by R. E. Charlewood, was much less praiseworthy. Two years earlier Mr Charlewood had timed this service with the piston-valve B3 No 6165 *Valour* on a load of 12 bogies, 404 tons tare, 430 tons full. The uphill work was poor and with more moderate downhill speeds the train took 86min 30sec for the 71·6 miles from the Rugby start to a signal stop at Pinner. Speed had fallen to 35mph at Catesby Tunnel and to 30½mph at the top of the 1 in 116 south of Aylesbury. The performance of the class could, at times, be good, but it was more variable than that of the four-coupled GCR engines.

The four-cylinder Class B7 was a mixed traffic version of the "Lord Faringdons", but they did a considerable amount of fast passenger work over the years. These engines shared in the running of the cheap fare excursions and details of a run timed in 1936 were given by D. S. M. Barrie in a letter to *Trains Illustrated* in 1951. B7 No 5459 had an 11 coach load of 364 tons tare, 385 tons full, on a schedule of 101min to Rugby. The train had an almost impossible schedule, for such a load, in the early stages and the engine dropped 4min, but it would have recovered all this had there not been a further delay for p.w. work in Catesby Tunnel. From Amersham Summit, passed at 28mph, the 45·5 miles to passing Woodford took 47¾min. This involved a maximum speed of 77mph before Aylesbury and minimum speeds of 48mph before Finmere and 45 at the top of the 4½ miles of 1 in 176 to Helmdon. This hill climbing was not far different from that of some of the runs by similarly loaded 4-6-0s during the 1948 Exchanges. A top speed of 76mph was reached at Whetstone.

In 1930 R. N. Clements recorded a run by No 5463 with a 10-coach load of 325 tons in the small hours of a Sunday morning on the down Newspaper. The start from Leicester was slow—there never seemed any special advantage uphill and at starting from the 5ft 8in wheels—but the mixed traffic engine reached 77mph at Gotham. The train passed Nottingham Vic. in 26min 30sec, 1½min behind schedule but after some good uphill work they reached Sheffield virtually on time in 75min 5sec. The up-grade work from Nottingham to Pilsley Summit was, perhaps the best hill-climbing attributable to this class of engine. The timing from Kirkby South Junction agreed to within a second with that of the similarly-loaded "Director" class engine *Princess Mary* timed by Dr Tuplin and published in *Great Central Steam* (Allen and Unwin, 1967).

The maximum speed of 77 at Gotham and before Aylesbury and 76 at Whetstone suggests that at around that speed the B7 was reaching its maximum. This corresponds quite closely to the rotational speed of the B3 at 85mph and the cylinders, valves and motion were similar. Dr Tuplin once recorded 80mph from a B7 piloting an Atlantic on the descent to Whetstone. And another was personally observed passing Loughborough at what must have been a similar speed with an Atlantic giving moral support on an Immingham Boat Special.

The large number of B7s made their use on fast trains more frequent than that of the other mixed traffic 4-6-0s. The only known timings of the "Glenalmond" class were with moderate loads between Leicester and Loughborough achieving the relatively modest maximum speed of 64mph. The B6 class seem to have left no published record but one was observed on the turntable at Leicester Central station after bringing in the express which arrived each morning after a 26min run from Nottingham. Arrival must have been punctual or nearly so. The return working was on a 24min booking and it is understood that these engines and the B7s were able to keep the booking.

The "Fish Engines" did little really fast work in LNER days, but they performed a fair amount of secondary passenger work.

There are two examples in the Charlewood notebooks of "Fish Engines" assisting on expresses south of Leicester shortly before the Grouping of 1923. The pilots helped the train engines, a "Director" in one case and an Atlantic in the other, to make fast climbs to Ashby Magna, but little fast running was required afterwards. At times the B9 goods 4–6–0s with their 5ft 3in wheels were called out on holiday specials, sharing the duties given to the "Pom-Pom" 0–6–0s.

The 4–6–0s from the GCR that entered LNER service did a good deal of useful work. They were not without merit, but it must be repeated that the best high-speed running was to the credit of the "Directors" and Atlantics. Little that the 4–6–0s did even in the field of uphill slogging, where they might have been expected to excel, could not equally well have been performed by the smaller engines.

CHAPTER SIX

The "Sandringhams"

Of all the 4–6–0s inherited by Gresley the GER 1500 class were the most generally successful. They may have been the best, but they certainly were not the biggest. Yet the demands of the GER were considerable, as its loads were heavy on a far from easy road. As standard LNER coaching stock was gradually introduced on to the GER, moreover, the tare load for a given carrying capacity was increased. New rolling stock was particularly essential on this line as road transport made inroads into passenger revenue, for GER journeys were not excessively long and hence it found competition from road motor coaches effective, especially after the 1926 Strike. When the lesson of the 1925 Exchanges had really sunk in, the need for a more effective use of steam was recognised. All this meant that the building of a new class of modern, efficient, locomotives for the GER was a priority for the newly-formed LNER.

The task of designing a suitable engine for the GER was not easy. The problem could not be solved by the *force majeure* of a Pacific nor could a large 4–6–0, built in the grand manner of Swindon, be accepted on to the very restricted main lines of East Anglia. It has been suggested that as early as 1925 a new taper-boilered 4–6–0 was being considered, but F. A. S. Brown in *Nigel Gresley, Locomotive Engineer* (Ian Allan, 1961) could find no solid evidence. Some help was given to the GER by the posting of a number of former GNR K2 class 2–6–0s, fitted with Westinghouse brakes, and the building in 1928 of ten more B12s fitted with Lentz poppet valves. The LNER design offices were fully occupied and Gresley followed the precedent set by Fowler on the LMS over the "Royal Scots" by deputing much of the design work to the North British Locomotive Co, who were asked to work out a design for a three-cylinder 4–6–0 suitable for the GER and incorporating as many Gresley features as possible.

The engine which emerged was alien to the basic theme of Gresley design; it was, in effect, a "Royal Scot" reduced in size and in LNER guise. The new 4–6–0 had divided drive, with the inside cylinder driving the front axle, whereas Gresley preferred the three cylinders all to drive the middle axle. The form of pure Gresley 4–6–0 would have taken is shown in a proposed design of 1935 illustrated in F. A. S. Brown's biography of Sir Nigel Gresley;

this would have been a shortened Pacific. The engine actually built was a 4–6–0 in its own right owing little to the GNR, but more to Darlington. The boiler had a round top firebox and its grate area, 27.5sq ft, was not much larger than the 26·5sq ft of the GER 1500s. Any superiority in performance could only be expected if the steam were used more effectively.

Steam distribution was by the Gresley derived motion placed behind the cylinders, which would have been impossible if the inclined rods of the inside motion of a true Gresley layout had been there. The position behind the cylinders had the slight advantage of eliminating the variable effect of the expansion of the outside valve rods. The outside valve motion was much like that on a Pacific, but the inside connecting rod was much shorter; this was not liked by those brought up in the Gresley school of thought, but it had to be accepted. The space between the middle and the rear axle was 9ft, longer even than that of the GWR "Kings", which were much bigger engines with a 34·3sq ft grate. The whole design was built to severe restrictions of axle load, total weight and length; much of the desirable solidity of construction of the pre-1914 4–6–0s had to be sacrificed.

The first engines were dual-fitted, with Westinghouse brake on the engine. The brake pump was located on the right-hand side of the smokebox. Despite scant overhang behind the rear driving wheels, a two-window cab was fitted, resembling that on the LNER K3s. To suit the short GER turntables the very short GER-type tender was adopted. The first ten, Nos 2800–2809, were built at the Hyde Park Works in Glasgow and delivery started in December, 1928. Further batches built between 1930 and 1935 came from Darlington. In 1936 more engines were built for the GCR and these had standard 4200 gallon tenders. The final example was built in 1937, giving a class total of 73 engines.

In 1937 the success of the streamlined "Silver Jubilee" express led to the introduction of a streamlined express named the "East Anglian" between Liverpool Street and Norwich. The schedule was not very enterprising, even considering the difficulties of the road, and the streamlining seems to have been applied mainly for publicity purposes. Two of the 4–6–0s were streamlined to resemble a small A4.

The new class were given the LNER B17 classification with a number of sub-sections. The batches originally built for the GER were named after country houses, beginning with the Royal residence of *Sandringham*; Nos 2848–2872 were named after football clubs and were nicknamed "Footballers". This was a good piece of publicity and it attracted the attention of young people who hitherto had hardly given the railway a look. There were a number of variations late as several engines were renamed after East

Anglian regiments and the two streamlined engines changed their
original football club names to No 2859 *East Anglian* and No 2870
City of London.

The troubles that beset the class were largely mechanical. The
long gap between middle and rear axles spread the weight over a
longer wheelbase, but there was considerable wear on the flanges
and axle boxes of the rear wheels. There was also grooving of the
frames and bending of the rear section of the coupling rods, especially on those engines used over the severely curved GER
lines. The crews complained of bad riding, excessive vibration and
axle box knock. Various attempts were made to improve and
lessen complaints but no permanent solution was ever found. The
first ten had nine plate springs, Nos 2810–2842 had 13 plate
springs and the remainder 15 plate springs; finally the entire
class was given 15 plates, but there was no real improvement.
In order to give some relief wedges were fitted to the coupled wheel
axle boxes of Nos 2848–2872 and R. N. H. Hardy has recounted
in *Steam in the Blood* how some inspired engine doctoring by Driver
Frank Cocksedge and the repair staff of Ipswich shed succeeded
in making No 61669 ride well; no universal cure for the class was
concocted. Where regular manning was backed by careful maintenance the bad riding was kept within bounds, but once the
engines were "common user" they became a daunting proposition
for fast running. Even the most careful attention could not keep
them in tolerable condition up to the time for a general repair;
the last 10000 miles were miles of tribulation.

The boilers had, of necessity, been lightly constructed to keep
within the weight limits and there were a number of fractures of
throat and wrapper plates. This trouble was never really cured,
but it was reduced during World War II by the reduction of boiler
pressure from the original 200lb sq in to 180lb. This took performance to a rather lower level, but as speeds were reduced as a
wartime measure and as passenger services had been reduced
considerably on the GCR this was of minor importance. Later some
of the engines were given 225lb boilers similar to those on the
B1s and these, at times, ran very well.

The GER 1500s and the GCR 4–6–0s were good riding engines
with comfortable cabs and their crews were not unduly impressed
by the B17s; the lightly-built cabs rattled compared with the solid
structures of the older engines. There were two designs of footplate.
Nos 2800–2847 had a floorboard without obstruction where men
could step across from one side to the other without tripping. A
single sheet fire screen was fitted on the driver's side of the firehole
to reduce glare in the cab. The firehole door was of the sliding
type, nicknamed by the men "the garage door"; this had to be
opened fully during firing with heat and glare making the footplate

somewhat uncomfortable.

Nos. 2800–2815 were dual brake-fitted; Nos 2816–2842 had steam brake on the engine with vacuum brake for the train; and the remainder had vacuum brake throughout. The brake apparatus was in each case placed on the firebox side in a position accessible to the driver whether sitting or standing. The earlier engines had tip-down seats on the cab sides.

The later engines, Nos 2848–72, were somewhat different but everything was not an improvement. The boiler protruded into the cab by the same 18in or so as with the earlier engines. The firehole door and mouthpiece was oval as in the GNR locomotives and no deflector was needed as an extension of the top flap opened well into the firebox, directing the secondary air downwards into the furnace and below the brick arch. The earlier engines with the sliding doors needed deflectors. After the "Footballers" left the GCR, most of them received the sliding doors. On the "Footballers" there were firescreens on each side of the firehole with a lid running in a slide in a manner similar to that used in fish and chip shops. This could be closed completely, shutting out all glare.

The "Footballers" had the "piano stool" type seats which were not popular. They were held to the frames by three $\frac{1}{2}$in studs in the base which constantly worked loose, allowing the seats to sway with the motion of the engine. In their old age, in post-war days, some of the cabs worked loose on the frames, aggravating the discomfort of an already rough engine.

At first there was another nuisance from the position of sand boxes for the trailing coupled wheels; these were placed inside the cab, which meant that the men had to ride side-saddle on their stools in a very uncomfortable and unnatural position. On the GCR there were complaints galore and inspectors were sent to ride and report. From September, 1936 onwards the engines went to Gorton Works in penny numbers, returning with the sand boxes below the cab outside the main framing. In this case there was a lasting improvement.

The B17s had the standard Gresley regulator and there was no trouble with leakage when standing with steam "blowing through", as was often a worry with the Pacifics and V2s. Generally speaking, the "Sandringhams" were good starters which kept their feet well. On the cross-country trains between Banbury and Woodford they have taken 14 bogies up the 1 in 86 of Chalcombe Bank without slipping or anxiety.

There was an automatic change-over valve on the exhaust steam injector and to operate this a steam pipe was led along the inside framing and underneath the top framing down to the change-over valve. A large nut secured this pipe to the valve which, when working, came under the control of main steam. Several instances were reported by drivers of the union nut packing blowing out, allowing a full bore of highly superheated steam to enter the cab, which immediately became untenable. This meant that the injector could not be used or there would have to be an emergency stop to hammer the offending pipe flat. Delay was caused on a number of occasions and taps or cocks were supplied by Gorton to be fitted in the sheds, though some engines were fitted when they passed through the shops.

One evening the fast 6.20pm down from Marylebone had to stop at one of the north London suburban stations so that the steam pipe could be dealt with. The Leicester driver had the idea of blanking the pipe off with a penny, but found that neither he nor his mate had the right coin. He borrowed one from a well-dressed spectator on the platform, who seemed interested and sympathetic, and in due course they were on their way. A few days later the Shedmaster called the driver in to congratulate him on his enterprise. The stranger who obliged was a high-ranking LNER officer and the ingenuity of the driver had not passed unnoticed. The driver treasured the bent penny for many years.

The original small GER tender was familiar on the Eastern as it was the same as that of the popular B12s, but it was not loved on the GCR. At first the B17s visited the GCR from Gorton or Doncaster, but when they were used on the through working from Marylebone to Manchester these small tenders had to be packed high for the run. A certain amount would be shaken off at high speeds and it was not wise to be near the platform edge at Wendover, Braunston, Whetstone, Quorn, Loughborough or Ruddington as these engines went through at speeds around the eighty mark. When the new engines of the "Footballer" batch were expected the GCR men hoped for a big improvement, but it was soon realised that they had only got the same engine with a bigger tender. In as far as the tender now held 4200 gallons of water and seven tons of coal it was better—there was no need for the high stacking of coal and the coal rolled towards the firemen more easily—but the engines rode just as roughly and many men criticised the new cabs as even more cluttered up, making movement more difficult than on the earlier batches.

Having enumerated so many points of criticism in the B17 design, is a relief to turn to the good side. The front end design was excellent. The same former GCR enginemen who condemned the engines so severely for their bad riding, maintain that on no occasion did any of the class give trouble with erratic exhausts or distorted valve gear. It was rare to hear a B17 seriously off its beat, which is more than can be said for the Pacifics or the V2s. It is claimed that the position of the conjugated gear behind the cylinders gave better steam distribution. Although the gear was less accessible in this position, it was less affected by expansion of the outside valve spindles and less vulnerable to smoke box ash. The result was that the "Sandringhams" had a quiet and purposeful beat and ran freely at high speeds. The coupled bearing surfaces were large and there was comparatively little trouble from overheated axleboxes. The B17s would start away smartly without slipping and a platform-end observer, who had spent some time on the GNR watching Pacifics and V2s, would get a pleasant surprise if he turned his attention to the GER or the GCR. In this particular facet of locomotive performance the honours did not rest with the bigger machine.

In BR days the B17s did little work on the GCR and were mainly found on the Great Eastern. They were given Class 4P, but those with 225 lb boilers were up-rated to Class 5P. In freight classification both classes were 4F for loose-coupled freights, but the 225 lb engines were allowed Class 5 loads on fully fitted freights. The class became extinct in August, 1960, when No 61660 was withdrawn. Ten of the class were rebuilt with two cylinders by Edward Thompson between June, 1945 and May, 1947; the last of these had disappeared by December, 1959.

Top: No 53, GCR two-cylinder mixed traffic engine, later LNER Class B6.
The Rixon Bucknall Collection

Centre: GCR mixed traffic 4–6–0 No 52 on down express excursion train
passing Rothley. This engine has a side-window cab. *H. L. Salmon*

Above: LNER Class B6 No 416 with plain cab at Nottingham Victoria.
T. G. Hepburn

Top: GCR 4–6–0 No 1167 *Lloyd George* with side-window cab passing Wembley on down Manchester express. *The Rixon Bucknall Collection*

Above: GCR four-cylinder 4–6–0 No 1169 *Lord Faringdon*. *The Rixon Bucknall Collection*

Top right: LNER Class B3 No 6165 *Valour* in early LNER livery at Nottingham Victoria at the head of the 2.20pm Manchester–London express. *T. G. Hepburn*

Centre right: Class B3 No 6164 with plain cab in later LNER livery at Nottingham Victoria. *T. G. Hepburn*

Bottom right: GCR War Memorial locomotive No 1165 *Valour* in GCR livery. *The Rixon Bucknall Collection*

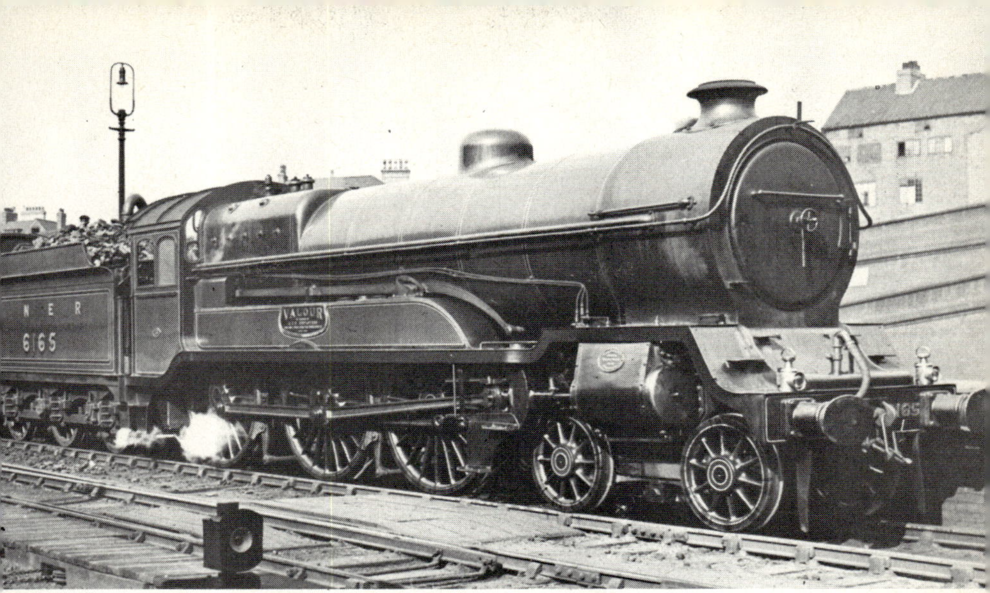
L N E R
6165
VALOUR

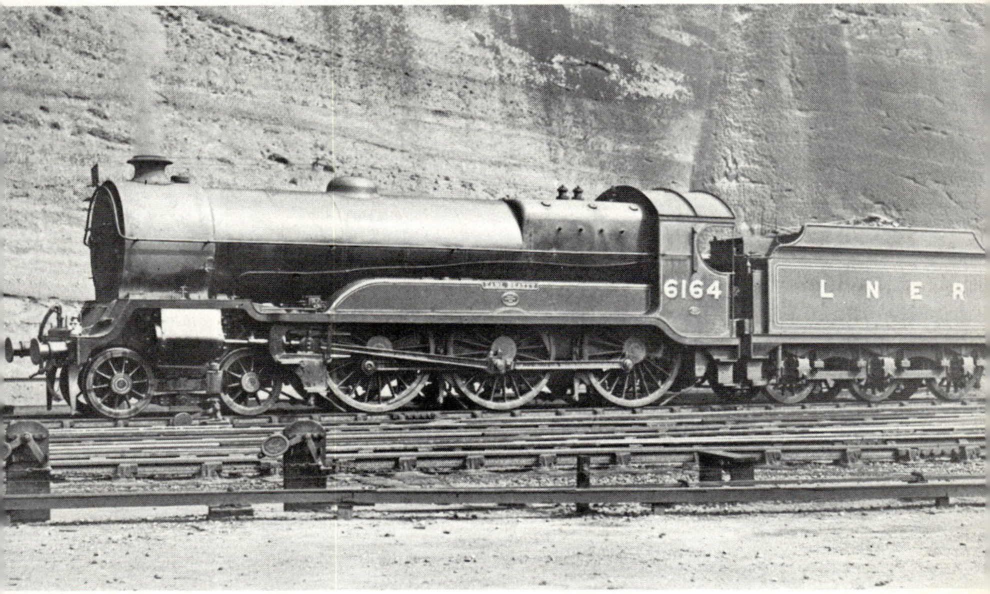
6164
L N E R

GREAT CENTRAL
1165
VALOUR

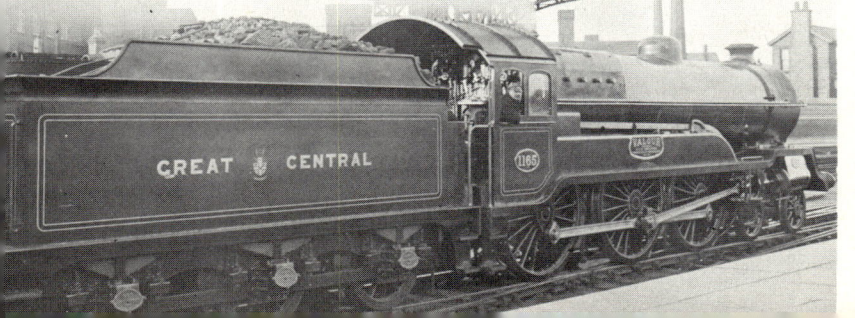

Top: Shortly after the grouping in 1923 No 1166 *Earl Haig* passes Hadley Wood with a 450 ton load on the 4pm from Kings Cross. This engine anticipated another four-cylinder 4–6–0, the GWR *Pendennis Castle*, by making good starts to Finsbury Park. *Locomotive Publishing Co.*

Above: No 6165 *Valour* hauling the down Edinburgh Pullman on the GNR main line. *F. R. Hebron*

Top: No 6166 *Earl Haig* with the original spring-operated Caprotti valves at Nottingham Victoria. *T. G. Hepburn*

Above: No 6164 *Earl Beatty* as rebuilt with the later type of steam-operated Caprotti valves at Leicester GCR. *T. G. Hepburn*

Above: B3 front ends; No 6166 *Earl Haig* with the Caprotti gear fully encased as first fitted and No 6167 with piston valves. Both are fitted with ''flower pot'' chimneys. Photographed at Nottingham Victoria as they wait for return excursion trains to Marylebone. *T. G. Hepburn*

Below: No 6166 as rebuilt with two cylinders and a 225lb boiler—Class B3/3. *British Rail*

Top right: Mixed traffic four-cylinder 4–6–0 No 38 in GCR colours at Guide Bridge on May 20, 1922. *W. H. Whitworth*

Centre right: Class B7 No 5475, built after the grouping to the LNER loading gauge, photographed with cylinder head removed at Doncaster Shed. *T. G. Hepburn*

Bottom right: The same engine in LNER colours renumbered 5038 with top feed removed and Gresley type sniffing valve, photographed at Doncaster Shed. *T. G. Hepburn*

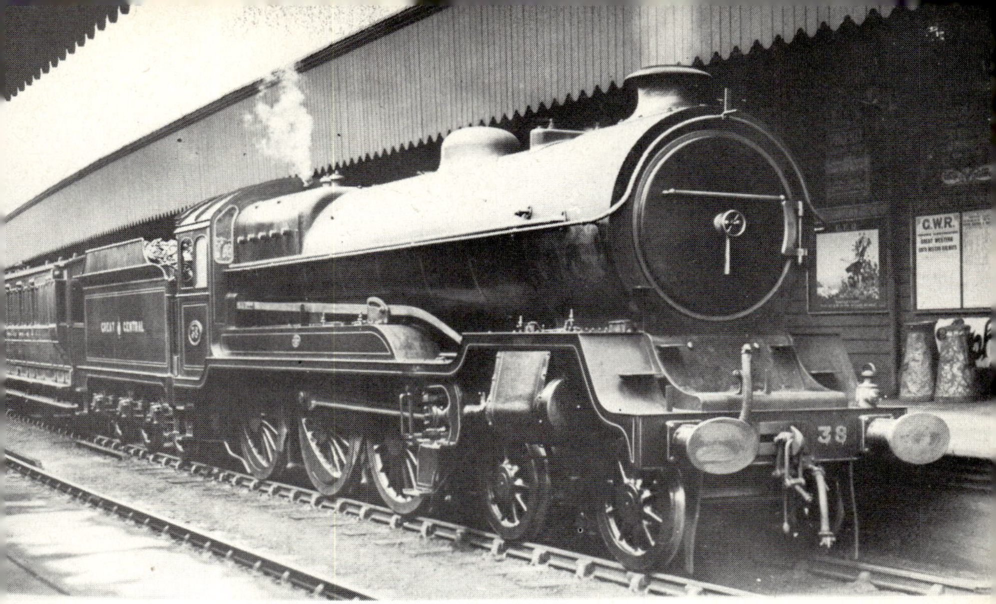
GREAT CENTRAL
38
G.W.R.

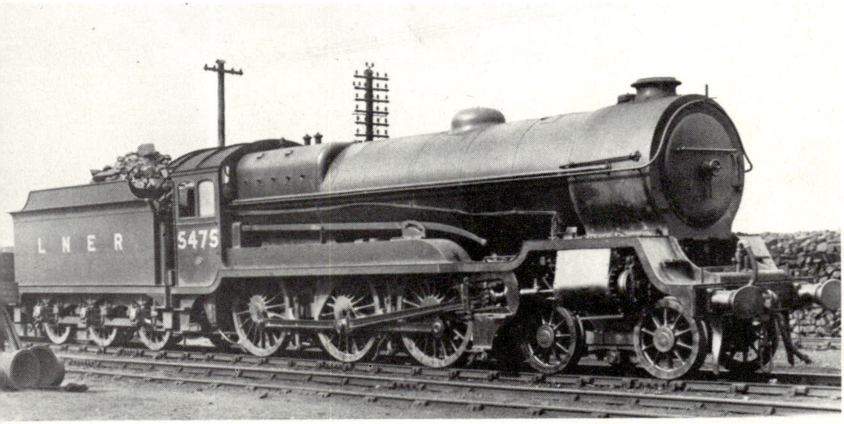
L N E R
5475

L N E R
5038

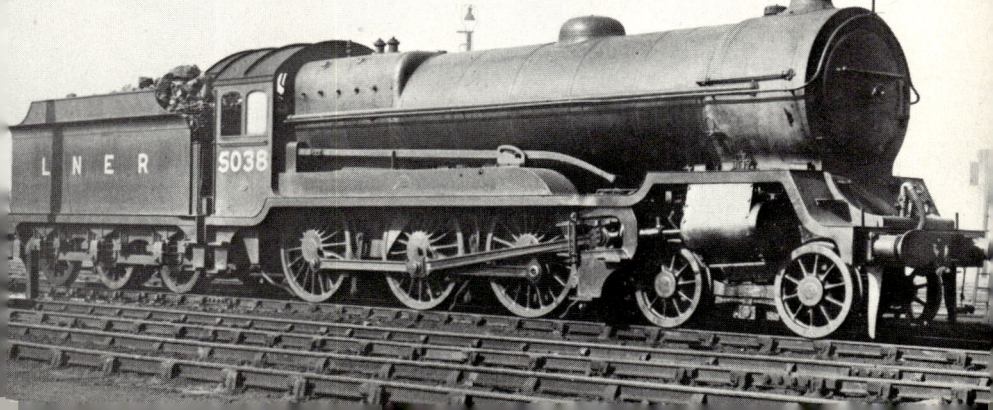

Above: GCR Class 9Q, later LNER B7, No 468 on a Southampton express near Rothley. *L&GRP No 1621*

Below: LNER Class B7 in the early days of grouping with top feed retained and number on tender hauling an Orient Line boat special past New Basford. *T. G. Hepburn*

Above: No 2800 *Sandringham* at the head of the "Eastern Belle" Pullman.
The Cecil J. Allen Collection

Below: The first B17, No 2800 *Sandringham*, at Liverpool Street.
Ian Allan Library

Top: Class B17 No 2803 *Framlingham* climbing Brentwood Bank with the "Day Continental". *Locomotive Publishing Co.*

Above: Class B17 No 2819 *Welbeck Abbey* approaching Littlebury on a Cambridge line express. *E. R. Wethersett*

Top: Class B17 No 2866 *Nottingham Forest* at Nottingham Victoria on an up Manchester express. *T. G. Hepburn*

Above: Class B17 No 2850 *Grimsby Town* passing Bulwell Common on the Bournemouth–Newcastle express. *T. G. Hepburn*

Above: Streamlined Class B17/5 No 2859 *East Anglian* on the pre-war "East Anglian" express. *E. R. Wethersett*

Below: No 61659 *East Anglian* makes a brief return to the post war "East Anglian" express which was more often worked by a B1. It is in LNER post-war green livery and is arriving at Liverpool Street on July 29, 1949. *R. E. Vincent*

Above: A line of LNER 4–6–0s, No 61606 *Audley End* with B1s Nos 61351 and 61353. *C. C. B. Herbert*

Below: Class B17 No 61652 *Darlington* on an eastbound "North Country Continental" at Spalding. *T. G. Hepburn*

Top: Class B17 No 61665 *Leicester City* returns to the GCR to work the "City of Leicester Holiday Express". It is leaving Leicester for Marylebone on August 14, 1956. *G. D. King*

Above: In woebegone condition, with nameplates removed, Class B17 No 61660 leaves Syston on a Peterborough–Leicester stopping train on April 8, 1960. *G. D. King*

Top right: Class B1 4–6–0 No 8301 as originally built in LNER wartime black. *British Rail*

Centre right: Class B1 No 1125 in post-war LNER green at Doncaster Shed. *T. G. Hepburn*

Bottom right: Class B1 No 61157 in BR black livery at the head of the up Hull fish train at Nottingham Victoria. *T. G. Hepburn*

Above: The down "Day Continental" ready to leave Liverpool Street headed by Class B1 No 61361. This engine is one of the batch built by the North British Locomotive Co with the smokebox numberplate above the upper hinge. *British Rail*

Below: B1 No 61159 passing Weekday Cross Junction on the up "South Yorkshireman" on May 10, 1949. *J. F. Henton*

CHAPTER SEVEN

The Performance of the "Sandringhams"

If an observer in pre-war days travelled as a passenger and used a stop watch he might quite easily and understandably have formed quite a high opinion of the B17 class. This would have been especially true if his travels were mainly on the GCR. If the same observer looked beyond the mileposts and the dial of his watch and indulged in a little railway field work, then his outlook would have widened. The observer who haunted platform ends and visited sheds, keeping his ears open, would have soon become familiar with other aspects of "Sandringham" class performance. In fact the running on the road gave little indication of the rough ride. It is greatly to the credit of the men who drove and fired the B17s that their record on the road was as good as it undoubtedly was.

The main aim of the design was to provide a more powerful engine for the Great Eastern section, but on the main lines of East Anglia they made rather a modest impact. A few years later they were introduced on to the Great Central and it was here between 1936 and the outbreak of war that they achieved their greatest success. It was inevitable that one of the first tasks to fall to the lot of the new three-cylinder 4–6–0s was the haulage of the "Continentals" between Liverpool Street and Harwich. This task was extending the GER 1500s to their utmost, so much so that when standard LNER corridor stock replaced the lighter GER vehicles an extra five minutes had to be added to the timing. When new, Nos 2803–2805 were sent to Parkeston shed to work the "Continentls" between Liverpool Street and Harwich. This task was to Gorton to work the "North Country Continental". The early timings of this train over Woodhead did not demand any exceptional hill-climbing capacity, but it was a long through run and drivers were wise in not flogging their engines at the start while the condition of the fire rarely encouraged heroics at the end of the 240mile trip.

The first recordings of B17s on the Liverpool Street to Parkeston Quay trains did not suggest availability of any more horsepower on the banks than had been the case with the 1500s, but the new engines were quieter, giving the impression of a shorter cut-off which should have argued a lower coal consumption. It was found that 24 per cent with full regulator would take a 350 ton train up Brentwood Bank in scheduled time. When new, the B17s put up

C

some quite good mileage figures of up to 6500 miles per month. At a later stage mileage figures were less favourable.

In 1932 the LNER made a number of accelerations and as a prelude laid on a number of fast experimental runs with the Pacifics. The trials were extended to the GER, with a number of fast test runs by No 2800 *Sandringham* on Sunday excursion trains with 295 ton loads. Net times of 121½min from Liverpool Street to Norwich and 113min in the opposite direction were achieved, while the 40·9 miles from Prittlewell, on the Southend line, to London were covered in 45min 39sec. The run to Cambridge was less notable, with a net time of 59⅓min for the 55·7 miles with a lighter load of 235 tons. This running was good as far as it went, but it did not suggest that a sensational general advance in standards could take place because of the introduction of the "Sandringhams". They had proved to be a most useful reinforcement to the GER motive power department, but they did not start a revolution. Alterations more radical than those of Thornton had to wait until the "Britannias" arrived in the 1950s.

The GCR saw "Sandringham" class engines from their earliest days. The Gorton engines stationed there for working the "North Country Continental" made running-in trips to Nottingham Victoria and to Leicester Central. In the early 1930s, B17s penetrated the GCR from Doncaster shed on through fish workings to Banbury, returning northward on the Penzance–Aberdeen train; Nos 2832, 2833 and 2835 were observed on this bookings. Nos 2816 and 2834 from Gorton made occasional trips up to London on the Manchester expresses, but by 1935 the Gorton "Sandringhams" were working with some regularity on the fastest workings such as the 2.15pm up and the 3.20pm down. The early timings of these engines did not indicate any great advance on the standard of running established by the 4–4–0 "Directors", but better things were destined to follow.

Much of the best running on the GCR was made by the men of Leicester shed with GCR Atlantics. The 6.20pm down from Marylebone was always a Leicester turn and the 7.30am up from Sheffield was worked throughout by Atlantics changing at Leicester before the 109min run up to town. There were a number of lesser trains with more intermediate stops, which, although not attracting the same popular attention, were very difficult assignments for engines and crews. Among these was the 5pm down, thought by many of the men to be a more exacting job than the more spectacular 4.55pm which preceded it on a 107min nonstop booking to Leicester.

One day in 1936 the afternoon stopping train from Nottingham was observed approaching Leicester with its usual D9 4–4–0 piloted by a new green 4–6–0, which, on investigation, proved to be No 2848 *Arsenal* with part of a dummy football below the nameplate. So it was that the "Footballer" era at Leicester shed began. This was a strange period of contradictions, with the stop-watch fraternity of travellers recording run after run of great merit but with the enthusiasts who haunted the platform ends and the shed yards hearing a sorry tale. Today the memories of Leicester locomotive men of the "Footballer" era are of passing through the valley of tribulation. It is greatly to the credit of these men, not only at Leicester but at other GCR sheds as well, that the public enjoyed such good running. It is also evident that there was some good in the design, for if the B17s had been complete failures performance and reliability would have gone quite to pieces. In 1936 the "Jubilee" class on the rival Midland main line had not got over their initial troubles and it was easy for a traveller on both LNER and LMS main lines to have concluded that the former group had the better 4-6-0s. Now that history can be seen in full perspective it may well be thought that the evidence of 1936 gave a premature impression.

The new B17s were a disappointment to the Leicester men in that they did not include more modifications to the original design. They had been led to expect an improved version, but all they got was the same engine with a bigger tender. Nevertheless, within a year, they had to their credit an impressive selection of first-class performances.

The famous 6.20pm from Marylebone was the most spectacular turn set to Leicester enginemen. In February of 1936 the slip coaches on the 6.20 were replaced by stops at Finmere and Woodford, but the time of 114min, hard enough over such a road of 107·6 miles, was increased by only five minutes. The stopping time at each station was a mere 30sec. The result was that an already difficult timing was made still more difficult. For a few months GCR Atlantics, which had maintained this service for so long, ran the retimed train which they could manage with up to eight bogies. The B17s, within their first year, showed their ability to keep time with 11 bogies. This meant very hard running with minimum speeds of 55–60mph up long stretches of 1 in 176 'and 90mph maxima downhill. As first re-timed, the 14·6 miles from Finmere to Rugby was allowed 16½min, but this proved too severe and the initial 59 miles from Marylebone to Finmere was reduced from 67½ to 66min to allow an extra minute to Woodford. The B17s could keep the new booking and the even time run of 34min from Woodford to Leicester, including two tempting downhill stretches, never imposed any difficulty. The good running standards shown by the records published by Cecil J. Allen confirmed the opinions formed by lineside observers in the Leicester area who had noted the good time-keeping.

Leicester engines and men also worked the 8.51am up to Marylebone in 109min; this was the 7.30am from Sheffield and was brought into Leicester by the B17 which had worked north on the down "Newspaper", with its 22min booking to Arkwright Street. Some of the semi-fast turns worked by Leicester shed were considered as difficult as the expresses; among these was the morning "Breakfast Car" train, which preceded the 8.51 up to London but which went via High Wycombe, and the 5pm down with its sharp start to stop bookings. At times extras were attached to these trains, which was an honour that the non-stops usually escaped. For many years good work had been done by the GCR Atlantics—in fact Leicester locomotive men in retirement will still maintain that these Robinson stalwarts could do all that the B17s ever did, but the published record, however, shows that the newer 4–6–0s had the advantage. It is a matter for regret that some Atlantic runs recorded in outline in Locomotive Inspectors' note books were not timed in detail.

When the B17s arrived in Leicester in 1936 they were assigned thus:

2848	Driver E. Cankwell	2852	Driver F. Sawbridge
2849	Driver T. Newall	2853	Driver A. Tetlow
2850	Driver W. Brooks	2854	Driver J. Webb
2851	Driver A. Bennett	2855	Driver E. Green

Later these workings became somewhat flexible to the extent that, when one of the best runs ever recorded by a B17 took place, Driver Webb had No 2848. There were the usual variations between individual engines. No 2848 *Arsenal* and No 2852 *Darlington* were considered to be among the best, but Driver T. Newall claimed that his No 2849 *Sheffield United* could run rings round the whole lot. He certainly had some good runs to his credit with 2849, including two timekeeping runs with 400 tons on the 6.20—one of these was published by the late Cecil J. Allen—and a year later a punctual arrival with 11 bogies was observed.

The good running by the Leicester men does not mean that the other sheds had lower standards. Neasden men worked the 2.32am down "Newspaper" with B17s instead of their usual B3 4–6–0s. The "Sandringhams", with a larger grate area and a more modern front end, could keep time more easily. They were able to observe the 24min booking for the 23·9 miles from Brackley to Rugby, which is something that "5267" never recorded during his long period of timing the B3s. Neasden engines and men worked the 10.5pm down "Mail", the train which in earlier days was handled for so long by GCR 4–6–0 No 195. The 10.5 sometimes loaded to 15 bogies, which meant that the B17 would take a pilot (this was no disgrace, as shortly before World War II Pacific No 2552 *Sansovino* was noted with a "Director" as pilot at the head of 16 bogies).

The Neasden turn on which the new engines made the least impact was the 4.55pm down, with its 108min booking to Leicester. On this the "Directors" and the Caprotti B3s fought a rearguard action for the old GCR, sharing the work almost up to the outbreak of war.

Gorton engines and men worked the 2.20pm from Manchester, which had the same 110min booking from Leicester to Marylebone as the 7.30am from Sheffield, and the 3.20pm down, allowed 109min from Marylebone to Leicester. The Gorton engine worked right through in each direction and the B17s remained on this job until Gorton received its first allocation of Pacifics in the autumn of 1938. Neepsend had a working through to Swindon. For many years this was a job for GN Atlantics, but in 1937 Driver Skelton was in charge of No 2863 *Everton* at the head of the 9.5pm from Swindon to York. The "Cheltenham Flyer" was much in the news at that time and it was booked to pass Steventon in 18½min from Swindon, but with a load of 215 tons No 2863 cleared Steventon in 17min 30sec with a maximum speed of 88mph; with 295 tons its time was 18min 42sec and the maximum speed 82mph. On special occasions "Castles" made faster starts—for example, Driver Street on No 5029, hauling 235 tons, got through in 16min 45 sec after a maximum speed of 95mph. This was one of the best "Cheltenham Flyer" runs ever recorded in detail, but the B17 had come very close to the normal timekeeping efforts of the "Castles". It is not for one moment claimed that the general record of performance of the B17s over the whole range of time equalled that of those redoubtable GWR engines, but in that one short period between 1936 and 1939 no better tribute to the LNER engines could be wished for than the fact that No 2863 pressed the "Castles" so closely.

To show the B17s at their best three logs are included. The first two were timed by the late R. E. Charlewood, one on the 3.20pm down and one on the 12.15pm down with a number of stops and sharp point-to-point bookings. It is believed that these two runs are here published for the first time. The third run has been published several times and this log is taken from *The London and North Eastern Railway*, by Cecil J. Allen (Ian Allan 1966); it was timed by Sir James Colyer Fergusson and, in view of the load, it is perhaps the best B17 run on record.

On the first journey the driver kept close to the booked time throughout. It would have been possible to reach Leicester in 106min or very slightly over with a faster finish. On the 25min booking to Nottingham No 2862 arrived in 25min 4sec or in 24½min net. The initial start was slow, but the minimum speed of 66mph over Barnston Summit after 75mph at Loughborough was good with 360 tons.

		Sched.	Min	Sec	Speeds
3.20pm Marylebone-Manchester, 23.7.38.					
No 2862 *Manchester United* **Driver Glover: Gorton Shed.**					
Load 10 336 tons tare, 360 tons gross.					
Miles		*Sched.*	*Min*	*Sec*	*Speeds*
0·0	Marylebone		00	00	
5·1	Neasden Junct.		9	15	
9·2	Harrow	14	13	27	slack
13·7	Northwood		18	02	
17·2	Rickmansworth	22	21	48	sl. 37½
23·6	Amersham		32	44	33½/36
31·5	MP 31½		40	18	52½
33·3	Wendover		42	15	72
37·9	Aylesbury	45	46	27	60 eased
44·1	Quainton Road	52	52	12	64/59
46·8	Grendon Junct.		54	48	
54·5	Finmere		61	49	56min
59·3	Brackley		66	22	
62·5	Helmdon		69	44	
69·1	Woodford	76	75	47	
71·5	Charwelton		78	14	
78·5	Braunston		84	07	80
83·2	Rugby		88	11	
90·0	Lutterworth		94	47	60/56
			eased		
103·1	Leicester	109	107	42	

The second was very good for a relatively heavy train over an undulating road and with very sharp start-to-stop timings. Time was not kept on the 12½min booking from Brackley to Rugby, but this was very difficult with 360 tons. If it was to be kept, even with loads lighter than 365 tons, a hard start and some skilled braking was called for. It was usual with a B17 on this booking to run with 40–45 per cent cut off as far as Helmdon distant, during which period firing would be continuous. Two of the best times recorded over this section were made by classes of engine with reputations on the GCR that left something to be desired. In 1927, B2 No 5426 *City of Chester* with a light train of 215 tons made the run in 12min 9sec—it was perhaps typical of the "Sir Sam Fay" class that this smart sprint took place during an otherwise moderate run—and in 1961 K3 No 61913 with 320 tons made the same distance in 11min 55sec.

Loads of up to 14 bogies could be worked by B17s on specials over the GCR south of Nottingham. One occasion when a heavy unusual train appeared was on Sunday, March 28 1937 when, in connection with a tour of Belgium organised by the *Leicester Mercury*, a train of 12 Pullman cars consisting of 10 third class cars and two Pullman restaurant cars was assembled. This substantial train, weighing over 450 tons tare, left Leicester behind B17 No 2865 *Leicester City.*

12.15pm	Ex Marylebone	Saturday 28/8/37			
No 2867 *Bradford* **Leicester Shed**					
Load	**10 344 tons tare, 365 tons gross.**				
Miles		*Sched.*	*Min*	*Sec*	*Speeds, mph*
0·0	Marylebone	0	00	00	
5·1	Neasden Sth Junct.		9	00	slack
11·6	Northolt Junct.	16	16	07	slack
18·7	Gerrards Cross		23	56	61/52·8
23·0	Beaconsfield		28	38	53·7/66
27·9	High Wycombe	34	33	59	
0·0	High Wycombe	0	00	00	
5·7	MP 22		9	50	44
8·1	Princes Risborough	13	13	04	
0·0	Princes Risborough	00	00	00	
5·6	MP 30		6	54	69
9·4	Ashendon Junct.		10	14	
15·3	Grendon Junct.	15	15	29	
23·0	Finmere		22	20	61/57½
27·8	Brackley	28	27	11	
0·0	Brackley	0	00	00	
3·2	Helmdon		6	31	
9·8	Woodford	12½	13	22	72 (before slowing)
0·0	Woodford	0	00	00	
2·4	Charwelton		5	07	
9·4	Braunston		11	28	81
14·1	Rugby	15	15	37	
0·0	Rugby	0	00	00	54/51
6·8	Lutterworth		9	07	
8·8	MP 114		11	08	
14·8	MP 108		16	06	79
18·8	MP 104		19	16	
19·9	Leicester	21	20	42	

Specials were in general easily timed, but that was hardly the case when the 8.51am up from Leicester with a load of 13 bogies weighing 437 tons tare, 465 tons full, was worked up to Marylebone by No 2848 *Arsenal* on the trip recorded in the following table:

Up Sheffield express 8.51am from Leicester to Marylebone Saturday 8th July 1939.

B17 No 2848 *Arsenal.* **Driver J. Webb, Fireman R. Hayes: Leicester Shed.**

Load 13.437 tons tare, 465 tons gross (including four-coach Immingham portion).

Miles		Shed.	Min	Sec	Speeds, mph.
0·0	Leicester	0	00	00	
4·7	Whetstone		7	45	50
9·2	Ashby Magna		13	55	42min
13·1	Lutterworth		18	59	73½ (beyond Shawell)
19·9	Rugby		25	12	63
24·6	Braunston		29	23	70
27·9	Staverton Road		32	42	—
31·6	Charwelton		37	17	44
34·0	Woodford	37	39	53	69½
37·0	Culworth		42	40	60
40·6	Helmdon		45	58	—
43·8	Brackley		48	46	79
48·6	Finmere		52	37	69
54·3	Calvert		57	03	80½/72
56·3	Grendon Junct.	56	58	45	63 (slack)
59·0	Quainton Road	59	61	14	71
65·2	Aylesbury	65	66	37	69
67·4	Stoke Mandeville		68	49	—
69·8	Wendover		71	54	—
71·9	MP 31½		75	05	39
74·3	Great Missenden	76	77	37	71
79·5	Amersham		82	33	55
81·5	Chalfont	83	84	26	80
85·9	Rickmansworth	87½	88	11	42 (slack)/48
89·4	Northwood		92	45	46/60
			pws		30
93·9	Harrow	97	98	47	—
98·0	Neasden S. Junct.	101½	103	12	68
100·1	Brondesbury		105	21	49
103·1	Marylebone	109	110	06	

Net Time 109min.

In 1939 one would not have expected to time anything significantly better than this with a "Jubilee" or "Patriot" on the LMS, with a "Star" on the GWR or with a "King Arthur" on the SR. The run was a perfect example of how an experienced driver, knowing his road and his engine, evened up the effort over the whole journey, uphill and down. A heavy-handed flogger might have climbed to beyond Ashby Magna rather more quickly, but would in the process have torn his fire to pieces; this would have lost him more time later in the journey than anything saved by running a "blinder" at the start. At about the same time Driver

Tetlow of Leicester brought an 11 coach 400 ton load up to Marylebone in a net time of 104¾min.

It might be claimed that B17s, on the form shown in the 1936–1939 period, could handle 12 bogies on the fast bookings south of Nottingham, but things were more difficult over Woodhead and on the severe grades between Nottingham and Sheffield. Here it would perhaps be fair to say that ten bogies was a rational limit. One of the best runs over Woodhead by a B17 was to the credit of Leicester's No 2848 *Arsenal*, which took a 10-coach train of 341 tons, tare, 360 tons gross, from the Sheffield start to Manchester in 57min 11sec or in 55¾min net. This meant that the 55min booking of the 4.55pm from Marylebone, intended for a normal load of six or seven bogies, was almost kept. Woodhead was passed in 33min 59sec from the start, speed was sustained at 40mph on the 1 in 120 and there was an immediate acceleration to 45mph on the short 1 in 160 to Barnsley Junction. From Wadsley Bridge to Dunford No 2848 would be maintaining approximately 1100edbhp and 1330ihp. It must be remembered that this was part of a sustained effort for 34min during which the train was lifted 760ft. A sustained edbhp of 1100 was good for a 77ton express engine at 41mph.

Work of this kind was not achieved easily. Experienced footplate men say that the B17s needed full regulator and 30 per cent cut off for hill-climbing of this sort. There would be no straightening of the fireman's back during the climb. Not even the best of steam engines produced high hps without burning some coal. Downhill coasting by the B17s at the regulation 25 per cent cut off was not pleasant. Bumping, banging, jarring and vibration persisted right down the bank and made many men wish they had never joined the railway service. Some men had their own methods of driving, intended to reduce the discomfort, but no lasting remedy was discovered. The introduction of Pacifics and V2s was welcomed and in this connection it must be remembered that the 180lb Pacifics which were transferred to the GCR in 1938 were better engines than the war-weary wrecks of A3s which the GCR received after 1945.

Among the B17s which were on the GCR for a short period was No 2870 *Tottenham Hotspur*, which after only being out for four months was taken into Doncaster Works to be streamlined to work the new "East Anglian" train. The rebuilding involved stripping down to the frames and No 2859 *Norwich City* was also chosen as being another East Anglian football team. *Norwich City* was first re-named *City of Norwich* and then *East Anglian* while No 2870 became *City of London*. The streamlined B17s had ample reserve power with the 230 ton "East Anglian" train. This was not streamlined externally; it resembled the "West Riding Limited" in the internal furnishings of its third class, but was different in the first-class section. From the point of view of comfort the train perhaps deserved its publicity, but it was not a high-speed job and could easily have been worked by a rebuilt "Claud" 4-4-0.

Although the "East Anglian" did not ask very much from the B17s in ordinary timekeeping service there were occasions when time recovery was necessary and fast climbs were made. One such occasion was when No 2870 passed Harold Wood at 66mph, Brentwood at 51½mph and topped Ingrave Summit at 49mph. A good run was timed behind No 2838 *Melton Hall* with a 370 ton train, which ran from Norwich to Ipswich, 46·3 miles, in a net time of 48¼min, almost keeping the "East Anglian" timing and this was followed by an even better run up to Liverpool Street with a net time of 74¾min. Ingrave Summit, which is easier from this direction, was topped at 52mph. The B17 with 11 bogies had almost equalled the time booked after the war for the much larger "Britannia" class Pacifics with nine bogies. During the last few years leading up to World War II the B17s had rivals on the GER in the shape of the rebuilt B12/3s, which shared their duties.

The B17s were rarely if ever used in Scotland, but the Doncaster engines worked at times up to Grantham on the same train that in earlier years had seen the "Imminghams" and the streamlined B17s had running-in turns to Grantham after rebuilding at Doncaster. On at least one occasion a Doncaster B17 was seen at the head of an East Coast express, when No 2832 ran as pilot to an ex-NER C7 Atlantic from York on a relief portion of the 1.20pm "Mid-day Scotsman". The pair was photographed leaving Grantham Locomotive Yard in pouring rain, but the picture is hardly good enough for reproduction. Before the outbreak of war B17s from Cambridge were appearing at Kings Cross on the "Beer Trains". The men did not consider them superior to the GN Atlantics on this job, but they had the advantage of being able to work from Cambridge either to Kings Cross or Liverpool Street at will, while the C1s were limited to Kings Cross.

As war broke out the passenger services on the GCR were cut drastically, while the increased number of Pacifics and V2s left little work for the B17s. They were transferred, mainly to the GER, but some went to Doncaster. Few tears were shed when they went. They reappeared on the GCR at intervals in the post-war world at times from sheds such as Colwick. One of the last express turns booked for a B17 by intention was the "City of Leicester Holiday Express" in August, 1956; it was worked by No 61665 *Leicester City*, but in the following year a B1 was in charge.

The final years of the B17s was a Great Eastern story and what might have been a tale of unrelieved gloom was brightened by the efforts of some devoted and talented men; these included shed-masters, locomotive inspectors, fitters, drivers and, most important of all, firemen. The GER turntables had been lengthened and the longer tenders built for the GCR allocation were equally welcome on the GER. So it was that some of the "Footballers" became, in the post-war period, star performers on the GER.

Ipswich Shed made a special effort to get some of its B17s into good condition. In 1952 it was given the task of running the Liverpool Street–Yarmouth "Easterling" non-stop over the 109 miles to Beccles. On the first run by Ipswich engines and men No 61668 *Bradford City*, driven by Driver A. Alderton, kept the "Easterling" on time after regaining 11min lost by signal checks. Later, No 61669 was entrusted to Drivers Cocksedge and Calver and by their efforts and those of the repair staff the engine was made a fast runner and a good rider. This was done by skilled manipulation of the wedges and by careful driving.

In *Steam in the Blood* (Ian Allan, 1971), R. N. H. Hardy has told how he found it desirable to have the "second eleven" at Stratford shed able to stand in for a "Britannia" class Pacific when needed. It had to be proved that it was possible for a B1 or B17 class engine to keep the "Britannia" timing. The engine chosen for the demonstration was No 61666 *Nottingham Forest*, once, in the days of its youth, a notable runner on the GC. In the hands of Driver S. Pittuck of Clacton and under the inspiration of Mr Hardy the Shedmaster, No 61666 reached Colchester in 54min from Liverpool Street against the "Britannia" booking of 56min.

There are no complete published test records of the B17 class showing all aspects of performance, but through the kindness of The Gresley Society it is possible to quote from an article by G. Goslin printed in *The Gresley Observer*. This article includes extracts from a test report on B17 No 1622 *Alnwick Castle* on the 3.40pm from Liverpool Street to Norwich on 22nd October 1947. The load was 425 tons tare, possibly 455 tons full. The test run was made with the dynamometer car, but no coal figures were included. No 1622 had been fitted with a boiler pressed at 225 lb and it was being tested for comparison with the two-cylinder Thompson rebuild of Class B2 and a B17 with boiler pressure reduced to 180 lb. The run was beset with signal checks and permanent way slacks, as was so often the case in 1947, but the engine showed a comfortable mastery over its load. Ingrave Summit was passed at a minimum of 27pmh on 24 per cent cut off with 1090 edbhp. On the easy stretches the engine ran on very short cut offs at one point as low as 7½ per cent.

The greatest interest centred on the start from Ipswich, where the engine was opened out to give a high edbhp.

A most interesting series of tests was made in 1936 between York and Darlington using the brake locomotive No 761 mentioned in the chapter on NER 4-6-0s. This was employed behind B17

B17	No 1622 *Alnwick Castle*. Load 425 tons tare, 455 tons gross.							
Miles	Location	Min	Sec	Speed mph	BP lb/sq in	SCP	Cut-off	Edbhp
0·00	Ipswich	00	00					
0·95	MP 69¾	2	45	36	210	200	40	1222
2·20	MP 71	4	30	47	225	215	31	1246
3·20	MP 72	5	39	52	225	210	31	1214

At 52mph the ihp would be in the region of 1500, but the effort was short-lived.

No 2861 in December, 1936 and January, 1937. These early attempts to examine the performance of a locomotive under conditions of constant speed must have been considered worth while as they kept an express engine out of traffic for three weeks. The most interesting trial was the full power test on December 17, 1936, when a cut off of 45 per cent was maintained with full regulator and an edbhp of 1360 was sustained in steady conditions at 42·5mph. The engine held its boiler pressure for 20min under these strenuous conditions of working. Thanks are due to Mr G. Goslin for these details and to Gp Capt Law for calculating the indicated horsepower as 1575. These figures are quite close to the 1951 B1 test result on a firing rate of 4000 lb of Blidworth coal per hour.

The *Gresley Observer* gave some interesting figures of mileage and availability as compared with some LNER engines of comparative size and power. The figures were for 1943, in the middle of the war, when no engine class was at its best. The B17s achieved a comparatively high mileage, varying from 34,308 on the GER to 38,889 on the GCR, but the number of days in sheds or shops was higher than that of the older two-cylinder types. Better mileage figures would doubtless have been made in peacetime.

The final days of the B17s were rather pathetic; they slipped away one by one, hardly raising a tear. The last one had gone by August, 1960, and no example of the class has been preserved. Yet they had known their moments of glory, especially on the GCR flyers before the war, and we should honour the men who made this possible.

CHAPTER EIGHT

The B1s

Sir Nigel Gresley died in office in April, 1941 at a rather depressing period of the war. The emotional uplift of the heroic days of the Battle of Britain had given place to a grim realisation that a long hard slog lay ahead with, as yet, no indication as to how or when victory would ever occur. Against the general background the death of a railway engineer made little impact on the general public, but those interested in the steam locomotive it was a shock, for it marked the ending of an era.

A moment's thought would have brought the realisation that, in any case, retirement would have not been far away. Further thought would have convinced everyone that hopes of a return to those days when the A4s with their streamliners disported themselves on the East Coast main line at three-figure speeds had little chance of early fulfilment. The task facing Gresley's successor was not an easy one, for it was already apparent that the problem of running a steam railway in wartime was formidable. An increased traffic had to be worked by a reduced maintenance staff and with a declining quality of coal. The days when an elite corps of brilliant but temperamental locomotives could receive favoured treatment were over.

The Gresley "big engine policy" had left the East Coast main line well provided for in terms of adequate power and very heavy loads could be hauled by Pacifics and V2 class 2–6–2s. The LNER had never been a wealthy railway and the money which had gone to the building of this large stud of powerful main-line locomotives had only been obtained by starving the secondary services of modern locomotives. The older types, including some of the pre-grouping 4–6–0s, had carried on well enough in peacetime, but the onset of wartime neglect made some of them jump rather quickly from an active middle age into shuffling senility. Gresley had recognised the need for more modern motive power for secondary services and just before his death the first of the V4 class of small 2–6–2 had emerged. This was an ingenious design with a remarkably wide route availability for so powerful an engine, but it would have needed the same careful maintenance as that given to a top-link A4 if it was to have given of its best. Nevertheless it was expected that, even under wartime conditions, the new V4 class would be multiplied as the standard LNER engine for secondary services. Initial trials of the first V4s had been carried out with every appearance of success.

The task of replacing Sir Nigel Gresley was given to Edward Thompson, Mechanical Engineer at Doncaster and after Gresley the most senior of LNER mechanical engineers. The name of Mr Thompson was unfamiliar to the general public, but he was well known within the LNER, having had experience at Stratford, Darlington and Doncaster. His early background was North Eastern.

A daunting prospect lay before him. The first essential was to keep the railway running during the emergency of war, but there was also the need to lay foundations for a range of standard locomotives, suitable for contemporary running conditions, which could be multiplied when peace returned. The new Chief Mechanical Engineer was 60 years old and could never have hoped to see his ideas through to fruition, but he was certain what had to be done—and also what should not be done.

One of Thompson's first acts was to cancel the order for ten of the new V4 2–6–2s. Nevertheless, he was quite clear in his own mind that a new standard mixed traffic design was badly needed. He did not, however, see much future for a small thoroughbred, as complicated as an A4 Pacific, cast in the role of general-purpose engine over the whole system. He was impressed by the success of the medium-sized 4–6–0s of the GWR "Hall" class and the Stanier "Black Fives", which had in a few years been so multiplied as to dominate the LMS scene. The "Black Fives" had perhaps been Stanier's greatest success, more significant to the railway as a whole than the relatively small number of "Coronation "class Pacifics. As a practical man, with experience of the operating difficulties faced by those trying to run the vital but unglamorous parts of the railway, Thompson realised that the A4s alone did not represent the railway. He sought to make better provision for run-of-the-mill traffic and, in retrospect, it must be admitted that he gained more success in this outwardly more modest but essentially more vital task than in the building of Pacifics.

He decided to build a new standard general purpose 4–6–0 which would be to the LNER what the "Black Five" was to the LMS. Its keynote was to be simplicity and ease of maintenance. As the war progressed new words entered the English language. One of these was "austerity", which meant the abandonment of many of the good things of life in favour of a limitation to essentials. In 1942 locomotive enthusiasts had received a shock in the appearance on the SR of a new 0–6–0, the repellent aspect of which was excused by the argument that it was admirably suited to wartime operating conditions. In the storm of protests which greeted this SR engine one of its defenders wrote: "Who knows what Mr Thompson's new austerity 4–6–0 for the LNER will look like?''. But the appearance of No 8301 *Springbok* from North Road Works, Darlington in December, 1942 was a most pleasant surprise, for the new 4–6–0 was a good-looking machine, not only the right shape for a steam locomotive but also completely LNER in appearance.

The reason why there had been no great departure from the outward appearance which had become associated with LNER locomotives was that, very wisely, a number of standard components had been worked into the new design. The boiler was similar to that used on the B17s, but the pressure was raised to 225 lb/sq in against the 200 lb of the "Sandringhams". The boiler was, in fact, the greatest departure from the GWR "Hall" or the LMS "Black Five", which both had taper boilers with Belpaire fireboxes in the Churchward tradition. The general trend of British practice had been away from the round top firebox and in favour of the Belpaire. The theory was that the taper boiler with its square firebox meant that the largest volume of water was at the rear end, where there was the greatest heat. The Churchward type of boiler was expensive in first costs, but its supporters claimed that it gained by good steaming and that it was cheaper in repair and maintenance costs. The LNER maintained that the simple round top boiler was cheaper to build: if there was any inferiority in steaming it was little more than marginal. There was some historical justification for this because one of the most remarkable boilers for steaming was the round-top boiler used, in saturated form, on the LNWR "Precursor" class 4–4–0s and in superheated form on the "Georges". In LMS days some of these engines had been rebuilt with Belpaire boilers, but with no better performance. This could, however, have been influenced by other changes in design. The rebuilding of the GER B12s with round-top boilers had been a great success, but this was not a fair comparison in that the boilers were larger and the front-end design had been improved.

The LNER under Gresley had been a three-cylinder line. Three cylinders gave good balancing with reduced hammer blow and that had been cited as the main reason why it had been possible to increase the axle loading of the B12 two-cylinder 4–6–0 to just over 54 tons in the three-cylinder B17 class. The new two-cylinder mixed traffic 4–6–0 had an adhesion weight of $52\frac{1}{2}$ tons, but the hammer blow was reduced by balancing only 30 per cent of the reciprocating masses. This had the effect, according to official statements published in 1947, that on test over bridges in the Eastern section the two-cylinder 4–6–0 caused slightly less stress than a three-cylinder B17 at the same speed. The price that had to be paid for the reduced hammer blow would, in theory, be bad riding. The new two-cylinder 4–6–0s were bad-riding engines, but it would be unrealistic to put all the blame on to the balancing because the B17s, with three cylinders and a better balance of reciprocating masses, were also bad riding.

In the great days of steam there was a tendency to over-dramatise the image of a locomotive designer. Enthusiasts would be inclined to imagine a man of genius and of unfailing intuition poring over figures and deciding with unerring instinct on the correct proportions. In actual practice other considerations prevailed, such as whether existing patterns could be used and what economies could be obtained from the use of standard components. One of the most successful 4–6–0 locomotives ever to have been built anywhere was the GWR "Castle", yet the design was not the result of intuitive genius applied to a drawing board; it was the outcome of circumstance. The original intention was to have built an enlarged "Star" with a No 7 boiler as used on the 4700 class 2–8–0s. The Civil Engineer rejected this design as being too heavy for the track in those days and a smaller boiler had to be built as a compromise. The fact that this design of accidental proportions proved to be so successful is a tribute to the innate elasticity of the steam locomotive, but it offends the once cherished belief that boiler/cylinder ratios are critical and that only the designer of genius could strike the correct balance. Of all locomotives the Thompson general purpose 4–6–0 was the supreme example of how an assembly of existing standard parts could make a successful design.

As the new 4–6–0s took shape on the drawing boards the elbows of the draughtsmen were, at every point of issue, nudged by the exigencies of war. The use of the B17 boiler meant that no new flanging blocks were required, and the increased pressure that a similar tractive effort could be obtained by using two standard cylinders. These two cylinders could be built from the existing patterns used for the K2 class 2–6–0s.

Modern ideas as to the correct size and shape of steam passages were introduced at a minimum of cost. The cylinders were 20in in diameter with a stroke of 26in, which compared with the slightly longer and narrower cylinders of the LMS "Black Five". The driving wheels were 6ft 2in diameter, as used on the V2 class 2–6–2s. The net result of the larger driving wheels and the shorter stroke was that a lower piston speed was a feature of the LNER design. In theory this should have helped at the highest speeds, but in practice there seemed to be little difference in the maximum and sustained speed capacity of the LMS 6ft 4–6–0s and the 6ft 2in 4–6–0s of the LNER and BR. The running plate was raised clear of the driving wheels and no splashers were needed.

The piston valves of the LNER engines were 10in in diameter with 6·66in travel and 1⅝in steam lap. The clearance volume, expressed as a percentage of swept volume, was 7·7 per cent, closely comparable with the 7·9 per cent of the A4 and V2. Doncaster and Swindon practice favoured the smaller clearance volumes as compared with the Stanier and Bulleid engines. In theory the reduced clearance volumes should have contributed to high cylinder efficiency and test results suggest that there may have been a marginal gain, but so many factors influence locomotive performance that it is unwise to make dogmatic claims about any single feature of design. The blast pipe nozzle had a slightly greater cross-sectional area than on the "Black Five". There was every prospect of the new LNER 4–6–0 proving to be a fast running engine in service.

The Gresley regulator, with its two pull-out handles, was replaced by the Thompson type with the long single handle working across the firebox backplate as on the majority of British locomotives. Both types of regulator had their advantages and their drawbacks. Both could suffer leakage at times from the stuffing box glands if the packing got hard or needed replacement. The trouble could be overcome by tightening the gland nuts of the Thompson type with a ⅝in spanner. When a blow happened there was danger in the Gresley type of steam spurting towards the driver's face along the cab side. On the Thompson type some but not all of the water which escaped might find its way on to the warming tray and in the most disastrous of cases into the tea-can. A little imagination directed towards what might happen to the water troughs brought engine crews to a depressing conclusion. The engines had steam brake with vacuum brake for the train.

The construction of the engines was made easier by the maximum use of fabrication and, steel casting was kept to a minimum; only the horn frames, the wheel centres and buffer sockets had to be cast. A new bogie was designed for the standard 4–6–0s. This was of the side-support type with the weight of the engine transmitted through spherical surfaces to bronze slippers. Helical springs controlled lateral movement to a greater extent than the swing link pattern of GN and Gresley pattern. There is no reason to blame the bogie for the bad riding, which was probably due to the combination of a number of causes including the balancing, and the long gap between centre and rear coupled axles. Whatever reason is put forward can lead to a counter-claim, citing an engine with similar features which gave no trouble or one alternative design which was just as bad. It can be stated with truth that no permanent solution was ever found.

The tender was the standard LNER design known as the Group Standard type. This tender had its origins in NER design and was developed by Darlington for the new K3 class 2–6–0s built there in 1924. In 1928 the stepped out-sides were replaced by flush sides and in this guise the tender really did take on a standard appearance, with its NER origins less apparent. This was the tender used on the later B17s, the V2s and the new Thompson 4–6–0s. Four of the class were fitted with modified tenders fitted with coal-weighing apparatus. Nos 61095 and 61210 were noted with self-weighing tenders, but there may well have been others.

At first the new engines were to be "Class B", without any number suffix, as the intention was for the standard locomotive class for each wheel arrangement to have solely a letter. Before long, however, came realisation that the engines intended to be "Class A" standard Pacifics were not good enough for standardisation and that several prototypes might have to be built before satisfaction was obtained. The classification then reverted to the earlier letters and numbers. The Class B engines became Class B1 and the former GCR 4–6–0s of Class B1 were re-classified B18.

The first B1 carried, on its smokebox side, a nameplate inscribed *Springbok* in honour of the visit of the famous South African General Smuts to Britain at a vital moment in the progress of the war. It was suggested that one engine be named *Utility*, but wiser councils prevailed. The engines were named after various species of antelopes and for a time the title "Antelope" class was encouraged; others called them "Springboks" but the enginemen and most of the interested amateurs called them B1s; and as B1s they are likely to remain part of locomotive history.

Many of the antelope names were excellent, but some, such as *Bongo*, were less happy. Antelope names were feasible while the class was small, but as numbers grew it needed an expert in African fauna to find new titles. As nationalisation loomed nearer a number of LNER Directors, like schoolboys carving their names on desks or on walls in their last week at school, sought immortality and a number of B1s received names which had nothing to do with antelopes. This was not as bad as the renaming of A4s with magnificent bird names after men who, however worthy in the Board Room, had not the grace and poetry of motion of the winged creatures. In the end, there were far more B1s than there were names and most of the class resembled their LMS counterparts in having numbers only. The final naming of a B1 took place in July, 1951 when No 61379 was named *Mayflower* to mark the visit of the Pilgrim Fathers' Association of Boston. After the ceremony *Mayflower* worked the Association's special train from Kings Cross to Boston. Later No 61379 was kept in specially good condition by Immingham shed and frequently worked through to Kings Cross on the morning express from Grimsby or from Cleethorpes to Birmingham on the through train.

The B1s were a standard class and there were relatively few modifications, rather less than on the LMS "Black Fives", which, however, had a longer history. One B1, No 61017 *Bushbuck* of

York shed, was fitted with a rear damper and it certainly showed plenty of "buck" when seen hauling a 12-bogie "Starlight" special up Staveley bank in fine style with a glow round its chimney top. Some of the later B1s had a slightly different footplating with a radiused curve on the underside, both at the front and the rear; these appear to have been in the batch built by the North British Loco Co. There were also some differences in the strap hinges. Some had smokebox straps reminiscent of GNR style set closer together, requiring the smokebox number plate to be placed above, while the others were more like LMS style straps more widely spaced, and on these the number plate was fitted below the upper hinge.

Electric lighting was fitted on a number of B1s. The principle was excellent, but bad maintenance outweighed the usefulness in many cases. There were two types. The Metrovic system had a switch box containing a number of spare bulbs which was attached to the cab roof just above the driver's head. It was quite easy to open the box lid to switch on whichever lights were needed. Lights were provided for the gauges, cut-off indicator and one to light the cab. A generator was attached to the left-hand trailing bogie wheel boss, but this did not quite come up to expectations and sometimes came adrift. The spare bulbs fitted the lamps on motor-cycles, incidentally! Stones equipment had individual switches for all lamps and moveable red shades, and wise enginemen made a practice of examining all switches and shades before darkness set in. The generator was steam-operated by a small turbine and was mounted on the running plate on the right-hand side of the smokebox. This was noisy, emitting a persistent humming when in operation. For a time an electrician visited the running sheds every Sunday to service the equipment, but his services were dispensed with after a time as part of an economy drive. At first it was intended that discs should be fitted above the small electric lamps to give the train headcode, but soon the old oil lamps were used as indicators and in course of time these became the source of illumination also. If the pre-war supply of labour had persisted after the war the experiment with electric lighting might well have been a success.

Some of the later B1s were fitted with the self-cleaning smokeboxes as used on the LMR "Black Fives". This was a wire mesh screen fitted inside the smokebox ahead of the blastpipe. Diaphragms and deflector plates were intended to ensure that ash which would normally drop to the bottom of the smokebox would find its way out through the chimney. This meant that there would be less need to clean out the smokebox by hand. It was not a popular device and it impaired the steaming to some extent, while the rain of hot ashes from the chimney would be a menace to clothing and eyes. Some visits to hospital eye departments were necessary and such things did not endear the apparatus to those who suffered, whether railwaymen, passengers or lineside dwellers. A number of adjustments took place, but the most popular modification—not approved by Authority—was the reallocation of the wire screens to a position on the waste dump behind the shed!

The bad side of the B1 class was its shocking riding and discomfort. The vibration could be so bad that sighting signals through the cab front windows gave blurred visions of dancing midgets in colour rather than of signals. The bucket seats were better than the stools of the B17s, but these worked loose on their moorings and in some cases broke away because of the vibration. The B1s suffered from what was called "steam knock", which disturbed the general riding as the big ends passed through the back and front quarters. Various attempts were made to improve this and there were numerous alterations to the balance weights. In some cases very thick copper joints were inserted between the cylinder end and cover. This made a noticeable improvement for a time, but when carbonisation got bad, back came the familiar thump and knock. The LMR "Black Fives" had similar trouble, which was tackled by moving the valve heads on their spindles, but as on the B1s the trouble eventually returned. The B1 axlebox sizes were 20 per cent less in area than those of the "Black Five".

On the good side the B1s were strong, reliable, good haulers, which were not scared of heavy gradients. Steam distribution was as good as any of their contemporaries. The B1 appears to have been rather better than the "Black Five" in working at short cut-offs and the results of the 1948 Exchanges suggest a greater willingness to pull the B1s up than was shown on the LMR engines. The Vulcan Foundry batch were considered by many of the men as being the best; with strong exhausts, they would notch up well, but like many strong engines they soon got rough. The North British Loco Co engines varied from batch to batch; some of the 1300 series had a bad reputation for being sluggish with woolly exhausts, while some would not notch up well and their indicators were suspect. Many drivers, of course, ignored the indicators and worked by feel and sound, but at 25 per cent some of the engines went "blind". When steam pressures fluctuated the B1s did not show it in their performance to the same extent as the B17s or the "Black Fives". Although both the B1 and the B17 had poor reputations for comfort, both classes could run well on the road and perhaps a majority of the men preferred the B1.

At first, in wartime, the number of new B1s built was small. Only 10 were turned out between 1942 and 1945; then, as post-war replacement of older engines proceeded apace, large numbers were ordered from outside builders to reinforce those built in LNER workshops. Finally there were 410 in the class. No 61057 was broken up after the Witham accident of March 7, 1950. The last was withdrawn in September, 1967 and one is certainly preserved while another may be. At first they were in wartime black but returned to apple green in the LNER post-war colour scheme. In BR days they received the LNWR-type black.

CHAPTER NINE

B1 Performance

At first little emerged as to the capacity of the B1s and, they were not called on to perform anything sensational during the war years. As compared with the "Black Fives", the B1s really were secondary engines because the LNER had large numbers of Pacifics and V2 Class 2–6–2s for their heaviest trains. The "Black Fives", on the other hand, were at times called out on heavy express trains of up to 16 bogies on the LNWR main line. The B1s took over a number of turns on the GER and GCR main lines, but in wartime, with additional stops and restricted downhill speeds, much of the work was of a semi-fast nature.

As peace returned it soon became apparent that there would be no quick return to normality on the railways. During hostilities many of the front-line express locomotives had been badly run down with the result that, on the LMS, the operating people seized with joy the new "Black Fives" and employed them on expresses because a new mixed traffic engine was better than a war weary, run-down, express engine. To some extent the GWR followed the same policy with their new 4–6–0 "County" class engines, but the reign of the "Counties" on the best "King" or "Castle" jobs was short-lived. The LNER had some new A2 class Pacifics and a larger stock of earlier large locomotives, so the B1s were not needed in the same way. They were, however, welcome on the GER and the GCR. The LNER re-introduced a number of named trains on these lines and on the GER the B1s were the favourite engines for the post-war "East Anglian", the new "Norfolkman" and the "Continentals". Although the schedules were 10min slower than the pre-war "East Anglian", with its six coaches and streamlined B17, the trains of the post-war period had to face far more speed restrictions and were usually half as heavy again. The "East Anglian" was restored in the winter of 1946 and the inaugural "Norfolkman" first ran in 1948 with nine bogies and a gleaming B1, which kept time despite six temporary speed restrictions.

On the GCR the equivalent of the pre-war 7.30am up from Sheffield was named "The Master Cutler" and although it was intended to be worked by an A3 class Pacific, in practice the B1s had to do quite a large share of the work. Although the schedule was slower than those of the pre-war GCR expresses the load was frequently 12 bogies or over. In the late 1940s the B1s were doing quite a lot of sound heavy work, but it was not of the kind which put them in the public eye. The "Black Fives", when first introduced, soon attracted attention by some heroic exploits when taking the place of larger express engines on the LNWR main line. There certainly were some occasions when B1s had to work 500 ton loads on the GNR, but there was never the coincidence of an exceptional effort and a recorder on board to give it the immortality that was gained by some of the GNR Atlantics which took over from Pacifics in pre-war days.

Through being introduced in peacetime, the "Black Fives" had built up for themselves a reputation for high speed. Whatever the capacity of the B1s for similar high-speed running, they had little opportunity in the wartime and immediate post-war world. Thompson's policy of building two-cylinder designs where possible was criticised by Gresley enthusiasts and it was predicted in print that the B1s would never be able to run at the high speeds regularly attained by B17s on such pre-war turns as the down "Newspaper" and the 6.20pm down. At the time the argument raged little could be cited in favour of the B1s, but a moment's consideration of the speeds attained by "Black Fives" on the pre-war XL timings on the Midland might have allayed doubts. The net results of all the considerations was, however, that the B1s went into the 1948 Exchanges as rank outsiders while the punters rushed to back the "Black Fives". There was some surprise as the results went up on the board.

The Locomotive Exchanges of 1948 brought great excitement into the lives of railway enthusiasts. They had greeted nationalisation with dismay as they feared standardisation and uniformity on an even greater scale than that which followed the grouping of 1923. One of the first events brought about by nationalisation was, however, one for which enthusiasts had craved. The GWR/LNER supporters in particular welcomed a replay now that they had bought some better players. The one disappointing aspect of the 1948 Exchanges was that full-speed running was far from being restored on the main lines and the largest express engines were perforce destined to run at speeds much lower than their undoubted potential. The mixed traffic engines, however, could run with speeds and power outputs much nearer to their maximums. In this category the contest was between the 4-6-0 "Black Fives", B1s and "Halls", which were all different expressions of the same general theme, and the larger SR "West Country" Pacifics. Clearly the SR engines, given the opportunity, would reach higher power outputs than the 4-6-0s, but the three smaller engines were well matched, with the "Black Five" and the "Hall" having the advantage of an honourable record of proved performance, while the

B1 was largely an unknown quantity. The B1 had only been able to run under wartime conditions or in the almost equally difficult aftermath, while the LMR and WR locomotives had enjoyed a few joyous romps in the piping times of peace.

Very little of interest happened to the 4-6-0s on the Midland main line to Manchester; loads were comparatively light, being limited to 325–335 tons, while between St Pancras and Leicester, where in pre-war days there would have been some exciting high speed running, schedules were slow and actual running was a case of hopping from slack to slack. The larger "West Country" Pacific made a few fast climbs, but nothing very exciting from the horse-power angle was achieved by any competing engine on the Midland. The running of the "Black Five" and the B1 seemed well matched, but the B1 gained some advantage in coal consumption.

The GCR section was one of the hardest that the competing mixed traffic engines had to face. It involved $5\frac{1}{2}$ hours of continuous steaming with the up gradients just as steep as they were before the war, but with the tempting down grades, where 80mph or over would have been commonplace before the war, limited to a miserable 70 which the 4-6-0s in general respected. The steeply graded section between Nottingham and Sheffield was infested with colliery pitfall restrictions. North of Sheffield there was a summit little short of 1000ft approached in one direction by a climb of 20 miles of 1 in 132 without a breather of any kind. On such a grade there is no substitute for good steaming. Only the large "West Country" Pacific was completely master of the job and its mastery was only achieved by hard continuous shovelling. The SR fireman is still spoken of with respect by GCR enginemen, especially by those who rode as pilotmen.

The LMS enthusiasts would very much have liked to see the "Black Five" achieve a resounding success on the GCR in view of the traditional Midland v Great Central rivalry. In the event the "Black Five" proved something of a disappointment and the driver came in for some accusation of "coal dodging" or deliberately losing time to save coal. GCR drivers who rode as pilotmen on the "Black Five" are convinced that the driver had a poor tool in his hand. This is supported by better records of "Black Five" running in later years. Little was published about the actual running of the B1 on its own road as the interest of recorders was, naturally, concentrated on the visiting engines.

When the report was published there was little evidence of the "coal dodging" suspected of the "Black Five", because it was run consistently on longer cut-offs than the B1 and it had attained a rather higher maximum drawbar horsepower—1,371—when starting from Loughborough. A better comparison with the B1 was at Crowden, where the B1 on 35 per cent cut off and full regulator reached 1238edbhp and the "Black Five" on 45 per cent and full regulator attained 1225edbhp at a rather lower speed of 34·6mph against 36·2mph by the B1. In spite of these shorter cut-offs the coal/dbhp/hr figures for the LMR engine on the GCR were slightly, but not significantly, lower than the ER engine.

Some of the best running of the entire test was made by the mixed traffic engines on the WR. The same "Black Five" was used, but seemed in much better condition as its work was consistently better than on the GCR. The work required of the mixed traffic 4–6–0s between Exeter and Bristol was, size for size, superior to that asked of the larger express engines. On the ascent from Taunton to Whiteball the B1 reached an edbhp figure of 1236 at 50.5mph, cutting off at 30 per cent with 225 lb pressure in the boiler and 205 lb in the steam chests. The published figure of 1283edbhp by the "Black Five" was at a different speed at a different point on the ascent and so is not directly comparable. On Dainton Bank, with the load reduced to 260 tons, the B1 recorded a maximum edbhp of 1207 at 35·8mph at a point well short of the summit. Again the "Black Five" figure was higher on the ascent and no significant comparison is possible. On Rattery Bank the rivals were recorded at much the same point and the difference between 1207edbhp for the B1 and 1200 for the "Black Five" lies within the limit of testing error.

On the return journey the worst bank to be faced is Hemerdon and it is unfortunate that the official report says little about the fastest climb made by any engine during the entire series of exchange running. The B1, ably driven by Driver Ratley, passed Plympton in 8min 39sec and from there climbed to Hemerdon Box in 6min 4sec with a minimum speed of 18mph. The good work was continued with a time of 7min 20sec from Totnes to Dainton Summit, again with a minimum speed of 18mph. The B1 had shown that the formidable South Devon banks held no terrors.

The running between Exeter and Bristol with 14 coach loads is of special interest. The climb from Exeter to Whiteball is best shown in a comparative table:

1948	"Black Five"	No 45253	475 tons	19·9 miles	24min 09sec
1948	B1	No 61251	475 tons	19·9 miles	26min 35sec
1948	B1	No 61251	490 tons	19·9 miles	26min 27sec
1948	"West Country"	No 34006	475 tons	19·9 miles	22min 19sec
1950	"Castle"	No 7036	500 tons	19·9 miles	25min 29sec
(ordinary service)					

The "Hall" running on its own road did nothing of particular note. The "Castle" run is added to give some indication, by comparison, of the high quality of the work of the visiting engines in 1948.

On the level section between Taunton and Bristol there was some fast running:

1948	"Black Five"	No 45253	475 tons	44·8 miles	46min 50sec
1948	B1	No 61251	490 tons	44·8 miles	47min 32sec
1948	"West Country"	No 34006	475 tons	44·8 miles	42¾min net

As on the climb to Whiteball, the "Black Five" would seem to have had a slight edge over the B1, but some of the difference was due to a more cautious stop and there was a slightly heavier load owing to a more crowded train. The maximum speed of the B1 on level track was 69mph against 71½mph by the "Black Five" and 75 by the Pacific; the B1's speed was, however, well sustained and it contributed to a fast time. Again the "Hall" did nothing of note, but there are runs recorded in ordinary service over this route where the WR engines have done much better work than their representative in the trials.

The hardest gradients of all were faced on the Highland section, for although they are not quite as steep as the South Devon banks these Scottish grades are much longer. There is no question of climbing a bank mainly on the impetus of a fast run at the foot. Each foot of altitude has to be gained by the sheer slogging of the engine and each pound of steam has to be paid for by coal on the fire. There is no question of building up capital in the boiler by starting with a big fire and a full boiler; long before the summit is reached capital is used up and the boiler lives on income. There is little scope for expansive working; it is a case of long cut-offs, full regulator and hard shovelling. It is no wonder that all engines returned higher coal/dbhp/hr figures on this route.

As might have been expected, both the 4–6–0 engines were completely outclassed by the "West Country" Pacific, but its success was bought by prodigies of firing by Fireman Hooker, who fed 63·2 lb/mile into the firebox of *Yeovil* during its test running on the Highland. One can only guess at the effort needed on the up grades. The 4–6–0s did very well, size for size, even if they were outclassed by the Pacific. The B1 reached a maximum edbhp of 1225 at 34½mph while working on 40 per cent cut-off with full regulator. On the climb from Struan to Dalnaspidal the B1 averaged 800 actual, not equivalent, dbhp for 18min with an average speed of 31½mph. At first the sensational climbs gave an impression that considerable economies could be expected if Pacifics were introduced to allow for greater unpiloted loads. In practice, however, slipping gave considerable trouble when the same class of "West Country" Pacifics were used on similar but shorter grades on the Somerset and Dorset Joint Railway. On special test occasions, the Pacifics could take heavier loads than the 4–6–0s, but in everyday service, in all weathers, they could only be trusted with the same loads. The "Black Fives" remained the mainstay of the Highland route, but the B1s gave good service on the shorter but even steeper grades of the West Highland section of the NBR.

The success of the B1 and the O1 2–8–0 in the 1948 Exchanges was a boost for the reputation of Edward Thompson, who had suffered great criticism for the rebuilding of the Gresley 2–8–2 *Cock o' the North* class and for the limited success of his Pacific designs. A consideration of the coal/dbhp/hr figures of the competing mixed traffic engines is a vindication of some of the things Mr Thompson was trying to achieve:

Average coal consumption on each region, mixed traffic engines.

	Black Five	B1	Hall	West Country	
LMR	3·71	3·34	n/a	3·80	lb/dbhp/hr
ER	3·29	3·32	3·84	3·90	lb/dbhp/hr
WR	3·39	3·96	4·11	4·28	lb/dbhp/hr
Sc R	3·90	4·01	n/a	4·77	lb/dbhp/hr
Average	3·54	3·57	3·94	4·11	lb/dbhp/hr

The difference between the 3·54 lb of the "Black Five" and the 3·57 of the B1 is not significant; it lies within the limits of testing error. The "Hall" was not allowed on the LM or Scottish Regions owing to width over the cylinders and it gave less than its possible best by being tested with Yorkshire coal, so a further series of test runs was made over its own road using Welsh coal, when coal consumption was reduced to 3·22 lb/dbhp/hr. If this figure is corrected for calorific value, it is roughly equal to the best "Black Five" and B1 figures. The very high coal consumption, both actual and relative, shown by the SR Pacific was due to some of its unique design features, which had contributed to its high power outputs but at a cost in fuel; it had nothing to do with the Pacific wheel arrangement as such. The ER O1 type 2–8–0 lies outside the scope of this book, but in as far as it had a similar boiler and cylinders to the B1 its performance becomes relevant. The O1 returned an average coal/dbhp/hr figure of 3·37 lb, the lowest of all the freight engines. The boiler of the B1 and the O1 had the same average evaporation rates of 7·68 lb of water per lb of coal. This gave them relatively low positions in the table of comparative boiler figures, but the good cylinder performance raised both designs to a comparatively good position in the tables of overall efficiency.

Following the 1948 Exchanges the reputation of the B1 class was further enhanced by the publication of a number of good runs on the GCR and GER sections. There was not the opportunity for the sustained high speed running of pre-war days on the GCR, but where restrictions allowed, the B1s gave evidence of being able to run as fast as the B17s. On the GER their running was very similar to the B17s in pre-war days, except in as far as track limitations prevented the full re-attainment of former speeds. New standards were destined to be established on the GER by the "Britannia" class Pacifics which, of course, quite outclassed both B1 and B17.

The performance of the B1 class again came in to the limelight after No 61353 was given a full series of tests on the Rugby Test Plant. Following tests on the rollers No 61353 was sent north to Carlisle as pilot to a "Duchess" class Pacific on the 10.40am from Euston. A number of road tests were then carried out over Ais Gill as confirmation of the results obtained on the Plant. Some modifications were made to the balancing of reciprocating masses in order to reduce oscillation on the rollers. In 1952 the full results of the test were published, along with the results of the testing of a WR "Hall" class 4-6-0 at Swindon. In view of the high reputation of the "Hall" class on its own road the figures were surprising in that the B1, on these results, appeared to be a much more effective engine in the higher speed ranges. These findings were received with surprise that approached dismay by the GWR enthusiasts, who were quick to point out examples of running by "Hall" class engines in ordinary service which appeared to be better than the test figures promised. This emphasised the fact that there are two factors to the final product of locomotive performance—design and operation. WR operation was excellent and very possibly the "Hall" gave of its best in everyday service more often than the B1. This, of course, was in no sense a denigration of the test results of the B1, which were very good. They are best shown in tabular form:

Dbhp on level track			Blidworth coal: 12600BTU/lb			
Coal lb/hr	2000		3000		4000	
Speed mph	40	60	40	60	40	60
B1	885	780	1220	1195	1400*	1390*
V2	820	675	1210	1080	1400	1260
BR7	790	610	1240	1140	1550	1460
BR 9F	900	700	1330	1170	1650	1510
BR5	830	700	1170	1100	1310	1240
"Hall"	780	560	1050	865	—	—

* Estimated from performance on South Kirkby coal.

These results show that the B1 was an extremely useful engine at speeds of up to 60mph within the limits of continuous hand firing and compared well with the other engines in the table. The figures for a coal rate of 4000 lb must be accepted with reserve, because the B1 was not tested at this rate with Blidworth coal. The figures given are an estimate based on performance with South Kirkby coal; they are a reasonable assumption but they are not actual proved test results. The B1 steamed remarkably well on Blidworth coal and this ability to burn low grade coal was a most useful feature in the post-war world.

The greatest interest comes from a comparison of the results of the B1 with those of the BR Class 5 of similar size and weight. The BR5, or the "73", as it is frequently called, was based on the Stanier "Black Five", but with a few small points of B1 design such as the 6ft 2in driving wheels and the LNER pattern slide bars. Basically, however, the BR5 was a modified "Black Five" and its performance was similar. An examination of the results leads to a very simple broad conclusion:

B1	BR 5
Good boiler	Better boiler
Better cylinders	Good cylinders.

These conclusions are supported by the results of the 1948 Exchanges. The "Black Five" and the BR 5 are not identical, but the differences are small. In 1948 the following comparative results were obtained:

	B1	"Black Five"
Water/dbhp/hr	27·64 lb	27·99 lb
Evaporation/lb coal	7·68 lb	7·92 lb
Coal/dbhp/hr	3·57 lb	3·54 lb

In this table, the "Black Five" has a slight superiority in boiler performance, but the near equality of the coal/dbhp/hr figures suggests that the B1's cylinders redressed the balance. It would have been unreasonable to have deduced anything very much from the 1948 Exchange results alone, but the support of the more detailed tests of 61353 justify a little more thought. It is unfortunate that the B1 was not tested to higher coal rates with the Blidworth coal; it might then have been easier to compare like with like. It would appear, however, that the B1 boiler dropped dramatically in efficiency as the firing rate was stepped up to the higher levels. For example, with South Kirkby coal, fired at the rate of 5350 lb/hr, the boiler efficiency was down to 44·9 per cent. The BR 5 reached a similar steam rate of 25000 lb/hr of feed water, but its boiler efficiency was still buoyant. Performance at these high firing rates is, however, of rather academic importance; they could be maintained under test conditions by two firemen, but were far above anything that could be expected on the road in everyday service.

It has been suggested that the LMR type boiler gained by having a Belpaire firebox which concentrated the greatest depth of water at the position of the greatest heat. Another suggestion is that the trouble came from an inadequate rear ashpan and the B1's lack of a rear damper owing to the position of the rear axle spaced aft behind the centre axle. This was carried over from the B17 design and has been cited as the cause of the bad riding of both classes. If steam had been continued, further research may well have suggested improvements to the B1 boiler performance at maximum outputs. As things were, the engines were of comparable efficiency to rivals of the same size and vintage at all normal operating levels.

An interesting point about the B1 test results was the fact that the engine reached its grate limit before its front end limit. The grate limit is the point at which any attempt to raise the combustion rate is frustrated by an increase in spark loss at least equal to the increased weight of coal fired; in other words, further additions of coal do not bring any more steam, only more coal going to waste. The test bulletins establish a definite limit for each class of engine on each grade of coal used, but in practice the point of limit is less rigidly defined; there could be some variation owing to different firebed thicknesses and damper settings. The degree of variation possible was, however, limited and the test house figure may be accepted within narrow limitations.

The "front end limit" is rather more arbitrary; this is the point at which the available combustion rate is limited by the draughting. If this rate was exceeded the exhaust got overloaded with smoke and the pressure began to drop. There were, even then, tricks by which the skilled crew could manage the engine so that a substantial burst of power could be held for several minutes; this would involve allowing the water level to fall. It would not be possible if the front end limit was very close to the grate limit. The BR standard designs were contrived so that front end limit was below grate limit in order to prevent uneconomic combustion rates, whereas the B1 was one of very few designs which reached its grate limit before its front end limit. It was almost as if the draughting was too efficient, were that possible. In practice, however, the limit could rarely be reached. A firing rate of 4000lb/hr was exceptional for a grate area of less than 28sq ft, but the B1s could produce a very high output for a short time and occasionally they did so.

The test report was in fact only a very detailed analysis of the performance of one engine; it was indicative of what might be expected from others of the class, but there was never any certainty that the findings would be translated into everyday performance. The bare bones of the test report need to be given some flesh in the shape of recordings in everyday service and by the comments of practical men who handled the engines everyday.

One of the hardest tasks set to any Class 5 engines in regular service was the booking of the GCR down "Newspaper", with its timing of 19min for the 18·9 mile climb from Calvert to Culworth Junction with a load of 390–400 tons tare, mainly of vans packed to the roof with newsprint with a high ratio of gross to tare load. This task meant that the large V2 class 2–6–2s had to be extended and even the hard pressed SR Pacific *Bude*, with its heroic fireman, only cut the booking by 1min. The best of the "Black Fives" and the best B1s could keep this booking and a retired GCR locomotive inspector who rode many times on both noticed no difference in the demands for coal from the two types of engine; both needed a lot. It would appear that not even this very hard job reached the point at which the boiler efficiency of the B1 fell violently. The test house report tended to be academic.

It is perhaps of greater significance to examine the test house findings at more moderate power outputs of everyday significance and here it is interesting to go back to George Jackson Churchward of the GWR, who established a criterion for a successful express engine in demanding a drawbar pull of 2 tons at 70mph. The B1 was able to reach this standard with relative ease at 23 per cent cut-off and a firing rate of 2000 lb/hr of the good quality South Kirkby coal or 2450 lb/hr with the Blidworth coal of more average quality.

The B1 emerged from the tests as a most useful mixed traffic locomotive. On moderate firing rates and at speeds of up to 60mph the dbhp figures compared favourably with any possible rivals and the B1s were strong enough in the higher speed ranges to deputise for express engines. This was all good, but it reflected the thermodynamic performance only. The mechanical design of the engines was also significant. They suffered from the need to restrict weight and reduction in axlebox sizes, while the need to reduce the reciprocating balance to lessen hammer blow meant that they were poor riding engines. This was made worse by the spacing of the rear pair of coupled axles. In comparison with the Stanier "Black Fives", the B1s were thermodynamically quite as good, but they were slightly less robust mechanically. This meant that there are less epic performances to record with the B1s than with the LMR engines. In any case, the fact that there were twice as many of the Stanier engines meant that there was twice the opportunity to achieve the spectacular. Nevertheless a number of excellent runs were recorded by reliable observers and they make a formidable collection which entitles the B1s to an honourable place in locomotive history.

The former GNR main line was well supplied with Pacifics and 2–6–2s, with the result that the B1s found relatively little work in conditions where spectacular results could have been expected. They took over the Cambridge train from Kings Cross, but restrictions on downhill speeds south of Hitchin prevented any restoration of the exciting running of the pre-war "Beer Trains". At first the B1s worked the Grimsby trains from Peterborough northwards, but later they ran through to Kings Cross and it was on these that the best B1 work on the GNR was recorded.

One of the best runs was timed by T. R. Pearson and published by the late Cecil J. Allen in *Trains Illustrated*. No 61190 had to handle a northbound load of 11 bogies weighing 378 tons tare, 410 tons full. Peterborough was reached in a net time of 76½min for the 76·4 miles; speed rose from 46mph at New Barnet to 47½mph at Potters Bar summit, while downhill the mixed traffic engine reached 88mph and averaged 80mph for 15·6 miles. This was work equal to the best that would normally be expected from a "Black Five" similarly loaded on the LNWR main line.

On the NER main line, too, there were sufficient large engines to cover most of the hard work. One of the best NER runs was made by No 61061, which took a 255 ton load from Newcastle to Edinburgh, 124·5 miles, in a net time of 125½min. In Scotland nothing was recorded which outclassed the standards established in the 1948 Exchanges. The B1s shared the work for some time on the West Highland main line and it is possible to find former enginemen who support the B1 against the "Black Five".

The most spectacular running ever recorded by B1 class engines in Scotland was, strangely enough, on a nearly level road. On a number of occasions between Glasgow and Edinburgh B1s reached speeds of 84–85mph on the 1 in 960 to Saughton Junction with loads of seven bogies. Speeds such as this with so little help from gravity mean more than higher speeds down steeper gradients and the B1 again came very close to the best "Black Five" and "Hall" class performances under similar conditions.

On the GER the B1s at first took over some of the best duties from the B17s with an apparently equal success. When the "Britannia" class Pacifics appeared, the 4-6-0s dropped to a secondary position, but there were, of course, times when they had to do their best to equal the Pacific timings. In many cases the 4-6-0s failed to do this, but some individual efforts reached a very high standard. A few examples of B1s coming very close to the Pacific bookings are the following runs taken from the writings of Cecil J. Allen in *The Railway Magazine* and *Trains Illustrated*:

No 61286	Load 315 tons Cambridge–Liverpool Street	55·7 miles	62min net
No 61302	Load 310 tons Liverpool Street–Cambridge	55·7 miles	60min net
No 61373	Load 320 tons Ipswich–Liverpool Street	68·8 miles	70min net
No 61089	Load 330 tons Liverpool Street–Ipswich	68·8 miles	73min net
No 61042	Load 245 tons Ipswich–Norwich	46·3 miles	43min net
No 61089	Load 330 tons Ipswich–Norwich	46·3 miles	47½min net

The run by 61373 from Ipswich to Liverpool Street was described by Cecil J. Allen, who knew the GER as well as any man, as a performance as good as anything he had ever known by a B1 on this line. It involved a minimum speed of 60mph at Ingrave Summit.

Top: Class B1 No 61251 *Oliver Bury* leaving St Pancras on the 10.15 Manchester express during the Locomotive Exchanges on June 15, 1948. *C. C. B. Herbert*

Above: Class B1 No 61353, after tests on the Rugby Plant, travels north for road tests over the Settle–Carlisle line. It is piloting Pacific No 46236 *City of Bradford* through Nuneaton on the 10.40 Euston–Carlisle on August 9, 1951. *J. F. Clay*

Above: B1 No 61086 with self–weighing tender about to leave Leeds Central station on a Liverpool–Hull train on September 5, 1952. *J. Woolfenden*

Below: Class B1 No 61370 with anemometer for testing the strength of the wind at March Shed after tests with No 61373 double-headed. Photographed on May 18, 1951. *H. N. James*

Right: Class B1 No 61244 *Strang Steel* climbing Glenfarg Bank. *W. J. V. Anderson*

Top: Class B1 No 61180 climbing Cowlairs bank with the up "Queen of Scots Pullman". *E. R. Wethersett.*

Above: Class B1 Nos 61199 and 61337 climbing towards Morley on the afternoon York–Manchester stock train on April 11, 1966. *M. Mitchell*

Top: Class B1 No 61366 leaving Leicester London Road on the 7.00 Cleethorpes–Birmingham train on Saturday, June 24, 1961. *H. A. Gamble*

Above: B1 No 61313 on the Southern; it is leaving Earlswood yard with a condemned wagon train on the first stage of its journey home after repair at Redhill following a failure on the Newcastle–Newhaven Car Sleeper train in October 1964. *G. D. King*

Left: With the overhead wires tracing a pattern of future motive power, Class B1 No 61171 makes a fine show of exhaust steam as it hauls a GER section stopping train up Bethnal Green bank. *J. A. Coiley*

Above: Class B2 No 1671 *Royal Sovereign*, the post-war LNER "royal engine". *E. R. Wethersett*

Below: Class B2 No 61616 *Falloden* piloting B12/3 No 61530 from Cambridge on an early morning local train to King's Lynn via St Ives and March on June 6, 1959. *G. D. King*

Above: B1 No 61306 renumbered 1306, painted in LNER green with pre-war shaded letters and named *Mayflower* with plates from No 61379, as now preserved at the Steam Railway Museum Carnforth. Photographed on July 25, 1971. *G. P. Cooper*

Below: Class B12/3 No 8572 under restoration at the North Norfolk Railway headquarters in Sheringham, September 2, 1973. *H. A. Gamble*

Although the approach to the summit from the north is easier than that from the south it includes a mile of 1 in 136 following more broken grades. The fast run with the seven-coach train from Ipswich to Norwich included a maximum speed of 88mph at Diss, perhaps a record for a B1 on the GER.

Some of the work by B1s on semi-fast trains was not to be despised. Two ascents from Brentwood to mp 19¼ were exceptional and compare favourably with the performance of a streamlined B17 on the crack train of the late 1930s.

No 61223 250 tons, Brentwood 56½mph, MP 19¼ 52mph.
No 61056 260 tons, Brentwood 53½mph, MP 19¼ 50mph.
No 2870 230 tons, Brentwood 51½mph, MP 19¼ 49 mph. (Pre-war "East
Anglian")

This selection of the very best of B1 performances over the GER show that, at the very top of their form, the B1s were a useful reserve fleet to stand behind the "Britannias". There were, of course, many other occasions when the 4–6–0s fell short of Pacific standards, but this was also the case when "Black Fives" deputised for "Royal Scots", or "Halls" for "Castles". If the schedules allowed Class 5 engines to keep Class 7 bookings under all conditions of loading and maintenance, then the larger engines would be underutilised. When the Class 5s were run at something approaching their test house maxima they could come very close and we must honour the crews who made this possible in normal operating conditions.

It was, however, on the GCR that the most significant performances took place, both as regards maximum power output and maximum speeds. Again all B1 performance was not at the same high level. The 19min booking of the down "Newspaper" over the 18·9 miles from Calvert to Culworth Junction has already been mentioned. The grisly hour at which this train ran repelled the recorders, but confirmation that a good B1 was capable of the uphill work is given by a run on the down "Master Cutler". The relevant portion is best tabulated:

No 61083 11 bogies, 376 tons tare, 395 tons full.			
Miles		min	sec	mph
0·0 Marylebone	00	00	
sig. stop and checks			
51·3 Grendon Junct.	72	18	—
53·3 Calvert	75	31	62½
59·0 Finmere	81	29	57½
63·8 Brackley	86	03	70 at bottom of dip 2 miles short of Brackley
67·0 Helmdon	89	13	59
70·6 Culworth	92	31	72½
73·6 Woodford (pass)	95	06	—

D

Work of this nature would require approximately 1050edbhp and over 1400ihp sustained for 20min. This would represent the best that would normally be expected under normal service conditions; higher hps could only be reached under test conditions with two firemen, except possibly for a very short period in ordinary service.

A similar power output at lower speeds was made by No 61182 on the climb to Woodhead before electrification:

No 61182 10 bogies, 336 tons tare, 360 tons full.			
Miles		*min*	*sec*	*mph*
0·0 Sheffield	00	00	
2·9 Wadsley Bridge	5	52	41
4·8 Oughty Bridge	8	37	42
6·6 Wharncliffe	11	08	44½
8·8 Wortley	14	28	38½
11·8 Willy Bridge	18	50	44
12·9 Penistone	20	37	—
0·0 Penistone	00	00	—
2·5 Bullhouse	5	21	41½
3·8 Hazlehead Bridge	7	10	43½
— Dunford No 2	—	—	—
6·0 Dunford	11	26	44½

Work of this kind would also need over 1400ihp, but the slower speed meant that less hp was needed to move the engine and tender, so that the edbhp would be around 1200. Similar hps on this bank were recorded by the B1 class engine in the 1948 Exchanges with a bigger load but at lower speeds.

Later the "Black Fives" were used on the GCR turn and turn about with the B1s in everyday service, with little difference in competence. Some of the work was better than that recorded in 1948. A comparison of the work of the two types under similar conditions is given in the following table:

	"Black Five" No 44855			B1 No 61116		
	11/379/400 tons			11/371/395 tons		
Miles	*Min*	*sec*	*mph*	*Min*	*sec*	*mph*
0·0 Leicester	00	00	—	00	00	—
4·7 Whetstone	7	20	56	7	04	57
9·2 Ashby Magna	12	25	53	12	03	53/51
13·1 Lutterworth	16	35	68	16	17	70
16·3 Shawell	19	25	78	19	05	76
19·9 Rugby	22	45	—	22	33	—

Both engines showed a comfortable mastery over the 25min schedule. There is little difference in the merit of the two runs and there are no published records of anything much better by either class over this section.

The ending of the through services to Manchester at the end of 1959 closed a chapter in GCR working, but some of the Nottingham semi-fasts had very fast start-to-stop bookings intended for diesel multiple-units. An exceptionally smart run on this service was made by No 61186 with a load of six bogies and a four-wheeled van. Leicester to Loughborough took 9min 35sec for 9·9 miles. It was rare for even time to be made by steam over such a short distance and with a rising start; even with a mere 230 tons it was good running to pass Belgrave, 2·3 miles, in 3min 22sec at 60mph. The maximum of 88mph at Quorn compares in interesting fashion with the test runs of the GN Atlantic and the *Sir Sam Fay* in an earlier chapter; neither of these engines equalled the initial start of No 61186. The journey continued with a time of 15min 30sec for the 13·5 miles start to stop. This was good, but it had been equalled plenty of times before the war by the B17s and the GCR engines. These GCR runs were all taken from the writings of Cecil J. Allen as published in various Ian Allan publications; they were recorded by Messrs Skelton, Cockman, Dyson, Hammersley and Norman Harvey.

Fewer very high maximum speeds were published from the B1 class engines, partly owing to lack of opportunity and possibly partly due to their poor riding. The suggestion that it was due to inability has, however, no foundation at all; the 84–85mph maxima on nearly level track in Scotland prove the opposite.

It is a great pleasure to be able to publish for the first time an example of really high speed with B1 class engines and doubly so in that the run was timed by G. J. Aston, a most reliable recorder. The run is not presented as an example of praiseworthy operating, but it occurred some time ago now. As it was dark, station and signalbox timings only were taken, but these tell us all we want to know and they are authentic.

Speed must have approached the 90mph mark through Loughborough and have fallen to little below 80mph at Barnston Summit; a maximum of 94–95mph was probably reached before Ruddington. Mr Aston knows of no special reason for the exceptional speed beyond Loughborough as departure from Leicester was only 1½min late. It was a wild enough ride in the train and the two Darnall crews on the engines must have been tough characters. Strangely enough, the highest speed ever recorded by B17 class engines on the GCR was also with a double-headed train that reached 92mph near Whetstone in 1937.

The B1s strayed from their own region both on a number of regular workings and on specials. There was a working through to Swindon and in the days in the late 1940s, when loads were still

Down "South Yorkshireman" 4.50pm Marylebone–Bradford Exch.					
Locos, B1s 61326 and 61087.					
Load, 10 vehicles 346/360 tons.					
Miles	Chains		Min	sec	Average pt to pt speeds
00	00	Leicester Central	00	00	—
1	07	Abbey Lane	2	27	
2	27	Belgrave	4	10	
5	03	Rothley	7	01	
					75·0mph
7	68	Quorn	9	16	
					84·7mph
9	70	Loughborough	10	41	
					84·4mph
13	24	Barnston Tunnel Sth Entr.	13	07	
					85·3mph
14	35	East Leake	13	58	
					88·2mph
16	67	Gotham Sidings	15	33	
					93·1mph
19	05	Ruddington	16	59	
					88·4mph braking
20	37	Wilford Brick Sidg.	17	56	
				p.w.s.	37½mph
22	47	Arkwright Street	20	59	
22	79	Weekday Cross	21	51	
23	36	Nottingham Victoria	23	57	
Schedule 26min Net time 21½min.					

heavy, Driver Banyard of Leicester, who later became an inspector, had to tackle a load of 16 bogies and two vans with No 1179. This attracted the attention of the Platform Inspector who remarked: "You've got a 'King' load there, driver". No 1179 managed in good style.

Following trouble with "Merchant Navy" class engines, motive power had to be imported to help out on the SR in 1954 and a number of B1s were sent to the SE&C section. It is hardly likely that the best examples were exported and there were very varied opinions expressed about the visitors. The voice of authority, however, came from Mr R. N. H. Hardy, at that time Stewarts Lane Shed Master, who suggested that they were hardly as bad as their critics suggested.

Towards the end some strange workings took place. On September 10th, 1958 No 61188 of Colwick Depot was noted by Horace Gamble in Leicester Midland shed yard; on the 14th of the same month it was on a Skegness train at Leicester Belgrave Road (GN);

and on the 17th at Leicester Central on a Nottingham train. During the late 1950s Leicester Central m.p.d. ceased to undertake repairs on locomotives and they were sent to Leicester Midland, less than 2 miles away as the crow flies but involving a journey of 50 miles by rail. When Peterborough Spital Bridge (MR) m.p.d. was brought under ER control B1s replaced the Midland 4–4–0s on the Leicester–Peterborough trains. For several years a B1 worked through Leicester Midland on the through Cleethorpes–Birmingham train and more appeared on holiday specials. It is thought that the last steam train at St Pancras was worked by a B1. Officially the last steam working was to have been an enthusiasts' special in April, 1965, but in the following December a B1 worked into St Pancras with a Christmas parcels train.

At various times heated arguments have raged, notably in the columns of *Trains Illustrated* and the *SLS Journal*, about the respective merits of the B1 and the "Black Fives" and almost everything relevant has been said by someone. On the road, each at its best, there does not seem to have been much difference.

CHAPTER TEN

Modifications and Rebuilds

As mentioned earlier the LNER was not a wealthy railway and Gresley was never able to undertake a "mighty re-stocking" comparable with that made by Stanier on the LMS. There was the need to make the best use of existing locomotives and a number of attempts were made to raise the efficiency of existing locomotives at a minimum of cost. In the early 1920s there were high hopes of a major breakthrough to higher locomotive efficiencies by the use of various forms of poppet valves. Poppet valves were derived from internal combustion engine practice and the 1914–1918 war had seen considerable advances in i/c engine design step by step with improved metallurgy. The minds of locomotive engineers turned towards adapting the new knowledge of steam practice. In theory the completely independent inlet and exhaust movements, made possible by poppet valves, promised great advances. In practice poppet valves rarely showed any sensational improvement on the best piston-valved engines in running and coal consumption, though there were hopes towards the end of steam that worthwhile increases in the mileage run before major repairs could be made.

In December 1926 a GER 4–6–0 was fitted with Lentz poppet valves. These were horizontal poppet valves driven by oscillating cams worked by the existing Stephensons Link Motion. Six more of the class received these valves between 1928 and 1930. It was reported that the first two conversions ran considerably increased mileages between heavy repairs and a batch of ten new B12 4–6–0s were built in 1928 with the new Lentz valves. These engines could easily be recognised by their raised running plates, which contrasted with the coupling rod splashers of the earlier engines, and by their plain chimneys.

At first it seemed as if there had been success, for early timings published by Cecil J. Allen earned from him the description of "sprightly". Among the men, especially those who worked over heavy grades, there was less enthusiasm. It was suggested that there were a number of mechanical troubles including cylinder cracking. The GER main line in the late 1920s and early 1930s was not the place for high speeds on the level or downhill and the full potential of the poppet-valve B12s for fast running was never realised. As things were, complaints from drivers sent inspectors ranging far and wide on their footplates and the final result was that a return to piston valves was ordered.

In 1926 Gresley experimented with a Worthington feed water heater on B12 No 8509 and between 1927 and 1934 he fitted 55 of the B12s with the ACFI feed water heating apparatus. This had the effect of reducing coal consumption by introducing water into the boiler at a higher temperature. Engines with this modification were easily recognised by the two drums on the top of the boiler behind the chimney where feed water was heated by exhaust steam before entering the boiler, impelled by a feed pump situated on the left-hand side running plate. There was a modest saving of coal, but against this had to be set the payments for the use of proprietary equipment and an added complication. The chief cause of failure of the ACFI heater in Britain was inadequate feed water treatment. Similar faults occurred on the later Franco Crosti system applied to BR 2–10–0s and feed water treatment was never tackled in the French manner. Engines fitted with the apparatus were nicknamed "Hikers" owing to the pack on their backs, though there is an alternative suggestion that, in the case of the B12s, the "Hiker" nickname originated in Scotland owing to the fireman having to take a step or so from tender to firehole because of the long cab. The B12s with Lentz gear were reclassified B12/2; there was no special classification for those with feed water heaters.

No 8519 had the single Kylala blast pipe fitted on July 1927, but little information seems available about its performance. Similar blast pipes were fitted to a number of LMS engines at the same period. The most successful rebuilding of the B12s, which came later, outclassed the various modifications.

While experimenting with the Lentz poppet valves, Gresley also decided to give a trial to the Italian Caprotti gear on a pair of the GCR four-cylinder 4–6–0s of class B3. These engines had a reputation as heavy coal burners and they had failed to show any improved running either on GCR or GNR metals over the GC and GN Atlantics or the GC 4–4–0 "Directors". In 1929 two of them, Nos 6166 and 6168, were fitted with the Caprotti gear. The gear was supplied by Beardmores and was identical with that used by the LMS on some "Claughton" class 4–6–0s of about the same size. There was a difference in the drive, however, as the simple cross drive under the smokebox had to be split in the case of the B3s owing to the low pitching of the boiler. These valves were spring-operated and the gear was basically of the type introduced by Arturo Caprotti in 1922.

In service these engines were well liked and easy on maintenance, although the valve springs tended to weaken and break under the action of high temperature superheated steam. There were failures owing to the breakage of the cam operating scrolls, which were cast iron, but this was overcome when bronze scrolls were fitted.

The front portion of the framing was removed to allow air to keep the camboxes cool when running.

There was some trouble with the springs. On one occasion, when a Caprotti B3 was on the fast 4.55pm from Marylebone in the hands of one of the most expert of Neasden crews, some of the valve springs stuck on starting and the get-away was hampered by steam roaring away to waste. The Leicester crew following on their Atlantic hauled 5pm were delayed all the way to Harrow, after which valves on the B3 re-seated themselves. The Leicester men had no more signals and they found on arrival at Leicester that the 4.55 had run in right time. The fireman, however, told of a difficult job in restoring the boiler to good behaviour after the fire had been torn to pieces.

The two Caprotti engines ran comparative coal trials with the piston-valve engines and our thanks are due to H. Phillips for details of the results. In ordinary service over the four years 1931–34 the mean coal consumption worked out at:

Caprotti valve 52·64 lb/mile   Piston valve 58·2 lb/mile

This was an advantage to the Caprotti engines of 9·6 per cent.

However, when working in the same link in comparison with a single-valve engine the results were:

Caprotti valve 52·64 lb/mile   Piston-valve 62·62 lb/mile.

This was an advantage of 15·65 per cent to the Caprottis.

Gresley was sufficiently impressed to order a series of trials on the same theme between March 9th and 14th, 1936, involving No 6166 and the piston-valved engine No 6169, both using the same grade of coal and with carefully measured results. The trains were the 8.45am down to Manchester and the 2.20pm up with loads varying between 163 tons and 277 tons tare. The results were:

Caprotti 42·2 lb/mile   Piston-valve 53·5 lb/mile.

This was an advantage of 21·9 per cent for the Caprotti engine.

Some indication of the running on individual trains was given by P.W.B. Semmens in an article published in *The Railway Magazine* containing extracts from the notebooks of the late Inspector C. Skinner. On one run, the 103·1 miles from Leicester to Marylebone were covered in 104min on a coal consumption for the whole run of 43·9 lb/mile with a load of 244 tons tare, possibly 255 tons full. The apparent conflict between this load and the official 227 tons was almost certainly explained by the addition of an extra vehicle, most likely a van, before the final stage of the journey. On three of the days the Caprotti engine regained time of the order of 5min, 2min and 3min. These coal consumption figures establish comparative values, but there would appear to be no figures surviving to relate coal consumption to the power output. The lb/mile figures appear high for such light loads, but the GCR was a difficult road and the trains were sharply timed.

While these trials were in progress, a complete reappraisal of the gear was being made and following the tests Gresley ordered two further engines of the class to be rebuilt. These were Nos 6164 and 6167, which were converted in 1938. In the revised gear the springs were eliminated and steam-operated valves were used as on all subsequent versions of the gear. The camboxes were strengthened with harder wearing surfaces and better oil sealing was provided. These engines are very well spoken of by retired enginemen who handled them in the early days of their conversion. They were good at getting away, including the difficult start from Marylebone. They reappeared on the cross-country trains from Woodford, including the Newcastle–Bournemouth which loaded heavily at weekends, and a period of test running under the eye of an enthusiastic Woodford Shed-master followed; but unluckily all the patient recording had to be put to one side and forgotten as the greater emergency of war dominated the scene.

Enough was known, however, to establish the point that the second pair were better all round than the first pair with spring loaded valves. The clearance volume of 13·4 per cent was considered to be still too high and Gorton prepared a design with reduced clearance volumes. The intention was, when the improved gear was perfected, to convert the whole of the B3 class and the entire B7 class mixed traffic 4–6–0s to Caprotti gear, but this bold scheme joined the carefully compiled records of the Woodford Shedmaster among the war casualties.

It may still be argued, however, that there was less to be gained by improving the cylinder performance of a class of engine with a suspect boiler than by scrapping the whole thing and replacing it with a more modern design with both boiler and cylinders representing the best that contemporary science could provide. When the war was over this policy was to dominate the LNER as large numbers of B1s were built to replace the older engines. Before then, however, when one of the B3s, No 6166, fitted with the earlier type of Caprotti valves, fractured its cylinders in 1943 and an expensive repair loomed ahead, it was rebuilt by Edward Thompson in a way which was almost a replacement but with enough of the original used again to justify the work in wartime. The engine was fitted with a B1 type boiler and cylinders and a new cab. The appearance of the engine was completely different and only the tender and buffer beam indicated its GCR origins. The running plate was raised almost clear of the driving wheels and the tiniest of splashers were fitted. The name disappeared at the rebuilding. The main difference from the later B17 rebuilds as Class B2 that was apparent was the different spacing of the driving wheels, which still followed the old B3 pattern. This could perhaps have been an advantage had the different position of the trailing coupled axle been used to allow for a rear damper.

This rebuild, with its modern front end, should have had a great advantage over the original engine, but little has emerged as to its performance on the road. The two cylinders gave better accessibility, but the rebuild was not such a good riding engine as the originals. We do not know how it would have behaved on the pre-war down "Newspaper"—in fact, one unfortunate happening is the chief memory of the engine. It stalled in Woodhead Tunnel and the driver, forgetting that the reversing screw worked in the opposite direction, put the engine into what he thought was full forward gear: thus, instead of drawing forward out of the tunnel, he set back into a following train. This is by no means the only occasion when something of the sort has happened in this country.

The rebuild gave Thompson some useful experience for his later rebuilding of some of the B17s as B2s. No 6166 suffered because it was the only representative of its class. Although some GCR drivers spoke well of the engine, which was classified B3/3, it was withdrawn in April, 1949 as No 1497.

Mr Thompson had previous experience of a very successful major rebuilding scheme while he was in charge at Stratford. In 1932 some of the GER B12s were getting badly run down with cracked cylinder blocks and life-expired boilers. In any case an expensive rebuilding was necessary even to restore them to their original condition, but for a slightly increased cost they could be thoroughly modernised. Clearly the latter course was the better investment. This was an opportunity which Thompson had long wished to come his way. He also realised that Gresley, who authorised the project, would halt further development if the engine failed. He received permission to cast new cylinder blocks and smokebox saddles for B12 class engines and to use a modified B17 boiler to replace some of the worn-out Belpaire boilers. These new ideas and a modernised valve gear were incorporated into engine No 8579. The new larger diameter, round-top boiler had a smaller nominal tube heating surface than the original, but there was more firebox heating surface, 154sq ft against an original 144sq ft, and the grate area was increased from 26·5sq ft to 31sq ft. The superheating surface was greater, 315sq ft against 202sq ft of the Robinson type superheater fitted in LNER days and 286sq ft of the Schmidt superheater fitted to 1500 and the first batch in GER days. A new Gresley-type cab was fitted and a shorter chimney and dome matched the height of the new Ross "pop" safety valves. The coupling rod splashers disappeared. The new rebuild promised a more solid basis for hopes of improved performance than had either the Lentz poppet valves or the feed water heaters of earlier modified engines. The really vital change was the increase in valve travel from $4\frac{3}{16}$in to $6\frac{1}{16}$in; although the valve diameter was reduced from 10in to $9\frac{1}{2}$in, the new arrangement promised a much more free-running engine with a lower coal consumption. It was classified B12/3.

It was not long before the excellent performance of No 8579 caused Gresley to order further rebuildings. The entire class would probably have been dealt with, but a number of B12s were needed for the GNSR to replace old 4–4–0s and only the B12s in their original condition had the low axle weight permitted on these lines. In course of time the boilers of these Scottish-based B12s passed beyond repair and they were replaced by new small round-top boilers; such engines were reclassified B12/4. These were not major rebuilds, like the larger-boilered B12/3s, and the Scottish engines kept their original valve gear and front end, but they lost the ACFI feed water heaters.

The B12/3s on their own road were the equal of the B17s in general running, though some drivers claimed that they were better. On the record there was not much difference and even in BR classification, made after the B12/3s were showing the effect of age, only the B17/6s with 225 lb pressure boilers were placed in Power Class 5 against Class 4 for the B12/3s and the other B17s.

The years 1935 to the outbreak of war were the heyday of the B12/3s. The track had been improved as compared with that of the 1920s and new higher standards of running were being established all over the country. An example of the work of a B12/3 with a heavy load was published by the late Cecil J. Allen in 1937. No 8556, hauling a 14-coach load of 431 tons tare, 460 tons gross, ran from Ipswich to Stowmarket, 11·9 miles, in 15min start to stop and this was followed by 38min 10sec from Stowmarket to Norwich, 34·4 miles. A maximum speed of 82mph was reached in the dip before Flordon. The start from Ipswich compares in interesting fashion with the test run of the B17/6 class engine described in Chapter 7:

		B12/3 No 8556			B17/6 No 1622		
		Load 431/460 tons			Load 425/455 tons		
Miles		Min	sec	Speed	Min	sec	Speed
0·0	Ipswich	00	00	—	00	00	—
4·85	Claydon	7	40		7	20	58
8·40	Needham	11	15	61	10	55	60
11·95	Stowmarket	15	00	STOP	14	28	PASS

Before a fully valid comparison could be made, it would have to be known just where the observer was situated in the B12/3's train; the B17/6 would be timed from the dynamometer car at the front of the train. The general conclusion is that there is not much difference in merit and if the B17 was reaching a maximum of 1500ihp the lighter B12/3 was at least as near as 1450ihp.

It becomes possible to compare three runs on which 4-6-0 engines almost equalled the "Britannia" timing of 74min from Ipswich to Liverpool Street:

	B12/3 No 8544	B17 No 2838	B1 No 61373
	Load 355 tons	Load 370 tons	Load 320 tons
Net time, 68·7 miles	74½min	74¾min	70min
Min speed MP 19¼	45mph	52mph	60mph
Max. speed, Brentwood	84mph	81mph	81mph

As might be expected the smallest engine, the B12/3, was slower uphill and faster downhill than its rivals but it was, for all that, a good effort.

One of the most exciting runs ever to have been timed over the GER before the advent of the "Britannias" was described by Cecil J. Allen. The engine was No 8535 at the head of a train of 280 tons tare, 305 tons full, on the second portion of the 3.40pm from Liverpool St to Cromer. The stirring happenings between Ipswich and Norwich are best tabulated:

B12/3   No 8535   Load 280 tons tare, 305 tons gross. Driver F. Mattin.

Distance		Min	Sec	Speeds, mph.
0·0 miles	Ipswich	00	00	—
2·5	Bramford	4	35	50
4·9	Claydon	7	05	60
8·4	Needham	10	30	65
11·9	Stowmarket	13	35	72
14·2	Haughley	15	38	61
15·3	M.P. 84	16	44	58
17·9	Finningham	19	12	70
22·7	Mellis	23	05	79
25·6	M.P. 94¼	25	05	90
26·3	Diss arr.	Special stop		
0·0	Diss dept.	00	00	—
2·5	Burton	4	20	50
5·5	Tivetshall	7	50	55
9·1	Forncett	11	07	74
11·7	Flordon	13	07	84/72
14·7	Swainsthorpe	15	30	75
17·0	M.P. 112	17	16	81
17·9	Trowse U.J.	18	12	30 (speed restriction)
		sigs		
20·0	Norwich	23	10	—

The special stop at Diss was because one of the train doors had blown open. The 72mph at Stowmarket had been reached up gradually rising grades while Haughley Bank, finishing with 2 miles of 1 in 131, was rushed at a minimum speed of 58mph. Had the run been made non-stop the 46·3 miles from Ipswich to Norwich could have been completed in 43½min or just inside the "Britannia" timing for a 9 coach load. The 90mph maximum before Diss is the highest that was recorded on GER metals before the Pacifics and diesels, but there are less well-authenticated stories of higher maxima with the rebuilt B12s. There is little doubt that they were very free-running engines.

In general terms, basing the comparison on everyday possibilities rather than the occasional exceptional run, it could be said that where the original B12s could keep a booking with nine bogies the rebuilds could be trusted with 11. In October 1938 the "Hook Continental" received a magnificent new set of coaches similar to those introduced in midsummer on the "Flying Scotsman". These raised the load to 485 tons, tare or 515 or 520 tons gross, a formidable tonnage to work over the GER line with relatively small 4–6–0s. The schedule had, however, been eased to 90min against the 82min of the 1920s. Before the outbreak of war the B12/3s had taken over the job from the "Sandringhams", but no published recordings appear to exist.

During the war the B12/3s were used on ambulance trains because their wide route availability allowed them to go almost anywhere. Many of these trains were very heavy and the sight of a B12/3 heading westwards from Cardiff in 1945, piloted by a GWR 2–6–0, is recalled. The B12/3s were, without doubt, the best inside-cylinder 4–6–0s ever to run in this country, but the weaknesses inherent in this type of locomotive were brought to the fore under wartime and post-war conditions of operating. The increased power of the rebuild raised maintenance problems more quickly than had been the case when the originals had led a less energetic existence before the war. After the war the best policy was to build new B1s for the hardest duties, so the B12/3s were downgraded to secondary duties. Many found their way to Grantham shed, where they could be seen trundling local trains of three or five bogies to Nottingham, Lincoln or Boston. One was once called upon to work a main line express following a failure and a considerable loss of time was the result whereas, on the form shown before the war, the job should have been well within its capacity. They visited Leicester London Road at the head of the "Swedie" from the M&GNR, sharing the job with the K2s which had replaced the "Clauds".

On their own road a rather happier situation persisted, especially where enthusiastic men, steeped in the best traditions of the old GER, had the encouragement of a Shedmaster such as R. H. N. Hardy of Ipswich. Among the B12/3s, which were maintained in first class condition, was the redoubtable No 61535 which, as 8535, had made the 90mph run before the war. This engine was given a cream cab interior and it was kept in excellent condition—so much so that, as Mr Hardy recalls in *Steam in the Blood*, it even received the praise of the formidable Motive Power Superintendent of the E.R., the late L. P. Parker, from whom kind words dropped sparingly. It is a happy thought that one B12/3 is to be preserved.

The B16s on the NE section were powerful engines with a reputation, like the B7s of the GCR, for burning a lot of coal. This may have been partly due to the steam reversing gear which had a habit of throwing itself into full gear without warning. When this happened at speed the sound could be devastating. Some drivers attempted to minimise this by running on long cut-offs with small regulator openings. A feature of the design was the monobloc casting for cylinders and valves which was regarded with some pride by the NER who, it is said, enlisted the help of Kitsons for its manufacture. The casting, however, meant an expensive repair in the event of a fracture. In 1937 Gresley rebuilt one of the B16s with new cylinders cast in one piece with the saddle, with valves above the outside cylinders driven by Walschaerts gear and the Gresley 2 and 1 motion for the inside valve. The engine was 9in longer, with the increase in the smokebox, and a new cab was fitted. The accessibility of the motion was much improved and the new front end permitted freer running and lowered the coal consumption. The screw reversing gear was welcomed after the vagaries of the steam-operated gear. The running plate was raised clear of the wheels. Seven engines were rebuilt in this way and they became Class B16/2.

In 1944 Thompson rebuilt a B16 with three separate sets of Walschaerts gear instead of the Gresley derived motion and between then and 1947 a total of 17 engines were converted, making Class B16/3. In outward appearance there was little difference between the Gresley and Thompson rebuilds because, with the rocking lever behind the cylinders, the 2 and 1 motion was not apparent. The Thompson engines, however, were fitted with left-hand drive and the position of the reversing rod—left for Thompson, right for Gresley—still forms a useful identification point when looking at old photographs. Both classes of rebuild were better than the original engines and it would seem that the Thompson engines were the more popular. When comparisons could be made, however, the earlier Gresley rebuilds had gone through the war and were past their best. The rebuilds did a fair amount of passenger work but few recordings are available. They occasionally visited Kings Cross from York, replacing V2s on fitted freights.

Thompson's general policy was not to use three cylinders if two could do the job and he intended to rebuild the B17s with two cylinders. The first of the "Sandringhams" to be so treated was converted in August, 1945. The rebuild was rather similar in appearance to the rebuilt B3/3 of a few years earlier, but the original B17 wheel spacing was retained. The boiler was of the B1 pattern with 225 lb pressure and the B1 20in by 26in cylinders were used. When this rebuilding first took place there was considerable criticism of the two-cylinder policy. It was suggested that two-cylinder engines could never be expected to rival the prewar speeds of the B17s on the GCR. The high speed record of the "Black Fives" on the LMS was cited in defence of Mr Thompson. One of the new rebuilds of Class B2 No 2871 was named *Royal Sovereign* and was kept in immaculate condition for working the Royal Train to Wolferton for Sandringham as required.

The trouble appears to have been that the original B17 frames were lightly built and they suffered from the increased thrusts of two cylinders as compared with the original three divided between two axles. In the words of one Running Foreman, the frames and running gear "took a belting". The B2s as a class had a good deal of frame trouble and no more than ten of the B17s were converted. Retired drivers voice all sorts of opinions about a B2's riding, varying from "better than a B1" or "better than a B17" to "worse than either". It is perhaps significant that the B2s spent most of their time at Colchester Shed and later at Cambridge; neither of which worked the most exacting turns. Nothing of any great note had been published about the performance of these engines; two runs described by Cecil J. Allen were disappointing. On test the B2 appeared better than the B17 with pressure reduced to 180 lb, but compared less favourably with the 225 lb B17/6.

Nevertheless it is possible to record one good facet of B2 performance. The "Royal" engine No 61671 *Royal Sovereign* was stationed at Cambridge with 61617 as a standby and both were kept in immaculate condition. No 61671 worked with regularity up to Liverpool Street in the morning and up to Kings Cross in the afternoon returning on the 17.52, sometimes double-headed. P. J. Coster was a regular passenger on the other 17.52 from Kings Cross with its N2 and a pair of Gresley Quad-arts. *Royal Sovereign* was the only engine he has known to catch an N2 on Holloway Bank. No 61671 with 10 bogies could be standing in Finsbury Park in less time than it took a Pacific, unless driven by Bill Hoole or Charlie Simmons, to run through. Possibly this strength was the cause of its frequent frame failures.

No B17 was rebuilt as B2 after March, 1949 and the class became extinct in December, 1959 several months before the last B17 was withdrawn. Under BR the rebuilding policy was discontinued in favour of replacement by standard steam designs and later by diesel locomotives. The last LNER rebuild to be withdrawn was a B16/3 in November, 1964. B12/3 No 8572 is preserved.

CHAPTER ELEVEN

The LNER 4-6-0s
in Perspective

To attempt to put the LNER steam locomotive in perspective is like trying to put the whole history of the steam locomotive in the 20th Century into logical form. The 4–6–0 was not typical of the LNER and it was only in the final years after World War 2 that the type was multiplied on a large scale for general purpose duties. Of the constituent companies only the GER was really a 4–6–0 line; the NER was largely an Atlantic line, while on the GCR, despite the large size and impressive appearance of some of its 4–6–0s, the majority of the fast trains were regularly worked by Atlantics or 4–4–0s. During the Gresley regime the only new 4–6–0 design that was built was the B17 "Sandringham" class and that was only intended for service in areas where Pacifics would have been too big or too heavy. There never was an LNER 4–6–0 which could be compared with the largest examples of the type to be found on other railways, but there might easily have been such an engine.

A large 4–6–0 design was prepared in 1935 for use on routes where Pacifics were not acceptable, but where it was hoped to run at speeds higher than could be expected from K3 class 2–6–0s and with loads heavier than could have been given to a B17. This design has been illustrated in *Nigel Gresley Locomotive Engineer*, by F. A. S. Brown, Ian Allan 1961, and elsewhere and it has been described as a "Super Sandringham". With respect it is suggested that a better description would have been a "Shortened Pacific", for the proposed engine would have been completely Gresley in conception. The cylinders would have been the same size as those used on the A4 and later on the V2, and all cylinders would have driven on the middle axle as with the Pacifics. The boiler would have been slightly tapered. It might have been expected that this large Gresley 4–6–0 would have matched the "Royal Scots" in performance and in course of time a modified version might have carried a double chimney. It is to be hoped that something might have been done to improve the riding; had this been no better than that of the B17s or the K3s it could have inhibited the fast-running qualities of the engine.

Although this engine was never built, it easily might have become the front-line express engine on lines such as the GCR. In the event the V2 class was multiplied and the large 4–6–0 design was abandoned.

It may fairly be claimed that the LNER inherited a stock of 4–6–0 locomotives from its constituent companies comparable in merit with any similar cross-section on lines other than the Great Western. The pre-grouping 4–6–0s of the LNER were, for example, roughly comparable with the 4–6–0s which were inherited by the LMS, although there is no evidence that any LNER 4–6–0 matched the high hps attained on test by the "Claughtons". The Hughes "Dreadnought" 4–6–0s of the L&Y were potentially a more advanced design than any pre-grouping LNER 4–6–0 as they had long travel valves. Unfortunately they were handicapped by leakage past the piston valves, which was not corrected until after anyone was interested in the future of the class. On the whole, however, it might be claimed that the LNER 4–6–0s were a fair cross-section of classical British practice.

On the NER the B13 and B14 classes suffered from being pioneers; by the time they entered LNER service they were long past their best and were mainly relegated to secondary services. The B15s were reasonably competent mixed traffic engines by contemporary standards, capable of giving the LNER many years of useful work. The large B16 class 4–6–0s were big powerful machines capable of much useful work at the cost of a fair amount of coal. They were not alone, however, in gaining nicknames such as "Miners' Friends" or "Blood Spitters" shared by other classes. The driving boxes were generously sized and the class enjoyed a fairly trouble-free life, apart from a characteristic wheeze which became apparent in their latter years owing to leakage from the outside-admission inside piston valve gland. As rebuilt by Gresley as B16/2 and by Thompson as B16/3 they were much improved engines. The B16/3s won good opinions on those former L&Y lines that were operated by the North Eastern Region.

The GER 1500s were, perhaps, the best 4–6–0s to enter LNER service at the grouping. Whilst not employing long travel valves, they had an excellent cylinder design with short direct steam ports without the restricted passages often found elsewhere. The 10in piston valves were of the Schmidt type with inside admission and had some similarity to those of contemporary LNWR locomotives. The standard of detail design and construction was very high at Stratford and, at this period, was perhaps equalled only by Swindon; a possible reason for this was that it stemmed from marine practice brought to Stratford during Adams' tenure of office.

The GCR 4–6–0s were perhaps the most interesting examples of the type inherited by the LNER, if only for their variety. On the debit side they tended to suffer from poor boiler ratios and draughting arrangements, from poor cylinder design with restricted steam flow and, in some cases—notably the "Sir Sam Fays"—from barely adequate bearing sizes. On the good side they were strongly built, good riding engines which had not been built down to a weight limit. This made them popular with drivers and even some firemen who, preferred to shovel more coal than to put up with the rough riding of more modern machines. Robinson introduced a very successful high-temperature superheater quite early on and this tended to overcome some other front-end deficiencies. His method of expanding the tube ends into the headers was widely adopted. Robinson looked after his enginemen well with good seating arrangements and later with side-window cabs. Had not World War II halted some promising experimental work, the B3 and B7 classes, with improved Caprotti gear, might have taken a larger share of the best work on the GCR. It is perhaps to be regretted that Robinson did not stop with the "Imminghams" and improved them in detail rather than building bigger 4–6–0s.

The LNER 4–6–0s were limited by the route availability classifications to which they were built. The B17 "Sandringham" class engines were not true Gresley locomotives, as they were built and designed by the North British Locomotive Co to a specification issued by Gresley from Darlington to conform with LNER standards. They had to conform to weight limitations imposed by the GER section, for which they were first built, and in order to spread the weight the spacing between the middle and rear axles was 9ft, which was more than the spacing of a GWR "King". This may have contributed to the bad riding also, and additionally the position of the rear axle made it difficult to fit a rear damper; which may have affected steam production at high firing rates. But the B17 boiler was well proportioned and steamed well at normal rates; it was later adopted for the B1s. They had drum smokeboxes and did not suffer the smokebox leaks which afflicted the contemporary LMS "Patriots". The axlebox journals and the inside big end were of Pacific size and this generous provision kept them relatively trouble-free and superior in this respect to the bigger engines.

The B1s also had to be built to a tighter weight specification than was really desirable and the maximum number of standard parts had to be included in order to assist wartime production. This resulted in a reduction of axlebox sizes and in reciprocating balance in order to reduce hammer blow. The bad feature of the B1, like the B17, was its poor riding. It may be asked why it was that engines riding as badly as the B17s and the B1s could have put up the high-speed performances detailed in this book. There is no doubt that these performances are authentic, but there is also no doubt as to the poor riding which often afflicted the engines of both classes. One can only praise the endurance of the crews who ran so well under such conditions of discomfort and perhaps assume that all the engines were not equally bad all of the time.

Thermodynamically the B1 was one of the best engines ever tested by BR. At moderate firing rates and at speeds of up to 60mph it compared well with any other engines tested at Rugby or Swindon. Possibly the boiler performance at the higher firing rates could have been improved by a rear damper, or there could have been further adjustment to tube A/S ratios or some re-draughting, possibly with a double chimney, to soften the blast. Against this can be claimed that correct use of a more complicated system of dampers might not always have been forthcoming and that maximum firing rates were rarely needed. Most engines in this country worked at moderate power outputs for most of their time. Possible alterations and refinements could have benefited many designs; that was the unfinished business of the steam era.

Some of the LNER rebuilds were excellent engines and the B12/3s were outstanding in this field, as successful as the brilliant Class D1 and E1 rebuilds of the SE&CR. The B16 rebuilds were useful engines, but the B2 project must have fallen short of the desired result, since it was cut short at ten engines.

It may be asked if the LNER would have been wiser to have built more 4-6-os. Would, for example, the proposed large Gresley 4-6-o have been a better proposition than such a large number of V2s? Would it have been wiser to have followed LMS practice and to have built just enough Pacifics for the cream of the traffic and to have worked the remainder with 4-6-o locomotives? The test reports suggest that it was the reverse of economical to have used a V2 on a train well within the capacity of a B1. Should there have been more moderate-sized mixed traffic engines at an earlier date? It is admitted that money was short, but ultimately the new engines had to be built at a time when prices were less favourable. Had a decision been made to build large numbers of medium-sized mixed traffic engines at an earlier date, the LNER would have been faced with greater operational difficulties during the war, when the large numbers of Pacifics and V2s proved to be so valuable. Had more money been available earlier the standard moderate-sized mixed traffic engine on the LNER would, almost certainly, have been a version of the V4 2-6-2 rather than a 4-6-o. Gresley does not appear to have had any undue infatuation for the 4-6-o type, even after the Stanier "Black Five" had been demonstrating its value for some years on the LMS. In true GNR philosophy there seemed to be no place for the 4-6-o; such engines were considered to be all right for "Geordies", "Swedies" or "Poggies", but they were not considered suitable company for such aristocrats as Atlantics or Pacifics.

The question of the correct proportion of large and small engines on a railway is largely an unanswerable one, for economic conditions may change radically during the lifetime of a locomotive. If Gresley is to be praised for his V2s, then Thompson also must be praised for his B1s, which had a definite role in the post-war world. It has been thought in the past that railway Chief Mechanical Engineers were masters of their own fate. That rarely was so; even Gresley, a man of strong will who had more freedom than most, was inhibited by limitations of space, weight and finance. Locomotive engineers did not have the choice between black and white, but of several rather dirty greys.

It is easy to suggest that a certain design feature which can be shown to have given good results was worthy of universal adoption and those designers who failed to do so might be condemned as lacking in wisdom. That may well have been true of the Church-ward front end, which gave something in the region of 30 per cent greater efficiency for little extra capital cost, but other features seemed to have less effect. The LNER kept to the round top firebox, for example, when others went over to the Belpaire box with seemingly justifiable results. Would the B1 and the B17 have been better with the extra steam space above the firebox at the hottest part of the boiler? Had this been adopted, however, the extra weight at the back of the boiler would have demanded a saving elsewhere and a taper boiler would have been required. The GWR enthusiasts would, of course, say that this would have been much better! But can we be sure? The smaller tube plate at the front end would have led to cramped tubes and a restricted gas area. All was not gain when either the taper boiler or the parallel boiler was chosen.

No one has ever built the perfect locomotive, but among the imperfect there are various pinnacles of relative success. The summit of thermal efficiency was reached by Chapelon and the summit of operational availability was, most probably, found by the New York Central with their "Niagara" class 4–8–4s running their phenomenal mileages. But the two paths to these particular summits would be marked by notice boards bearing the words: "Unsuitable for Englishmen". Our own designers had to face their own particular hazards and they had to find their own paths to success. Some of these paths proved to be more stony than others. Against such a background the LNER 4–6–0s must be judged; the best of them were never so good as not to disappoint occasionally and the worst of them were never so vile as not, occasionally, to give a surprisingly good performance in the hands of a skilled and determined crew. In this respect their story is the story of the steam locomotive.

Technicalities apart, the LNER 4–6–0s leave fascinating memories of stirring sights and sounds: of, for example, the three-cylinder beat of a B16 in full gear raising the echoes as it ascended Micklefield Bank with a heavy Scarborough excursion; of the "Hook Continental" with its B12, on an equally heavy load but with very different beat, on Brentwood Bank; or a "Lord Faringdon" rending the peace of suburbia in the small hours as it climbed to Amersham in a welter of sparks and noise with the down "Newspaper"; of the pre-war 6.20pm from Marylebone with its tough Leicester crew taking the knocks as its "Footballer" went swinging past the island platform at Whetstone at 90mph; or perhaps the finest memory of all, of a B1 with a V2 load on the up "Car-Sleeper", taking the route via the Midland's Beighton Junction and over the former LD&ECR "Clog and Knocker Line", bellowing into the night and filling the air with strands of "copper wire", dirty, unkempt and rough—yet master of the job and capable of taking the train through to London. This was the stern reality of working a railway by steam.

Appendices

1 LEADING DIMENSIONS

No absolute accuracy of finality is claimed for the appended tables of dimensions. Published dimensions are notoriously unreliable and often bear no relation to the actual dimensions of individual engines. Cylinder diameters as built are soon changed as the cylinders are bored out. Wheel tyre diameters are turned down. Boiler heating surfaces can vary with different batches of boilers, particularly when built at different works. More important, in this connection, is the fact that individual draughtsmen use different methods of calculation of areas which can vary with no real change ever having taken place. This applies particularly when allowing for the effects of radii at corners etc and differences between inside and outside tube diameters. In calculating superheating surface it is usual to take the inside diameter of the tubes but occasionally figures based on the outside diameters have been quoted and these have led to misleading comparisons with engines of the same general type on other railways.

Boiler heating surfaces are not, in themselves, significant. The really important dimensions such as boiler free gas areas, tube A/S ratios, and percentage of air space through the grate are rarely quoted. Superheating surface area can bear no relation to actual steam temperature. The number and spacing of elements, the A/S ratios and the distance of elements from the firebox tubeplate are far more important. On test it has been shown that, in some cases, the smokebox gases can actually cool the steam despite the high "superheating" surface.

An example of misleading dimensions quoted in this book is the high figure of 2817sq ft of total heating surface of the B2 and B8 classes as first built. This figure is 300sq ft greater than the nominal heating surface of a GWR King, which had the ability to produce over 1000 more hp. Better steaming was obtained later on the "Sir Sam Fays" and "Glenalmonds" from modified boilers with a total heating surface 500sq ft less than the original engines.

LEADING DIMENSIONS
NORTH EASTERN

Class		Cylinders			Driving Wheels	Working Pressure	Heating Surface sq ft			Grate Area	Weight tons		
NE	LNER	No	Dia	Stroke	Diameter	lb/sq/in	Tubes	Fire-box	Super-heater	sq ft	Engine	Adhesion	Tender
S	B13	2	20in	26in	6ft 1in	200	1640	130	—	23·7	63	47	39
SI	B14	2	20in	26in	6ft 8in	200	1639	130	—	23·7	67	52	40
Super-heated	B13	2	20in	26in	6ft 1in	160	1373	130	390	23·7	63	47	39
Super-heater	B14	2	20in	26in	6ft 8in	175	1373	130	390	23·7	67	52	40
S2	B15	2	20in	26in	6ft 1in	180	1226	144	545	23·7	71	53	39
S3	B16	3	18½in	26in	5ft 8in	180	1672	166	437	27·0	78	59	46
—	B16/2	3	18½in	26in	5ft 8in	180	1672	166	437	27·0	79	59	46
—	B16/3	3	18½in	26in	5ft 8in	180	1672	166	437	27·0	79	59	46

There were some variations in heating surface between various engines of Class B16.

Class B16/2, B16/3 8ft 5in between rear bogie and leading driving axles. Class B16 (reclassified B16/1) 7ft 8in.

Class B16/2 Gresley 2 and 1 gear.

Class B16/3 3 separate sets of Walschaert's gear.

LEADING DIMENSIONS
GREAT CENTRAL SATURATED ENGINES AS BUILT

Class		Cylinders			Driving Wheels	Working Pressure	Heating Surface		Grate Area	Weight tons		
GC	LNER	No	Dia	Stroke	Diameter	lb/sq/in	Tubes	Firebox	sq ft	Engine	Adhesion	Tender
8	B5	2	19in	26in	6ft 1in	180	1620	130	23·6	63	48	48
8C	B1	2	*19in	26in	6ft 9in	180	1777	133	26·3	67·6	52·5	48
8F	B4	2	19in	26in	6ft 7in	180	1777	133	26·3	70·7	52·5	48
8G	B9	2	19½in	26in	5ft 3in	180	1777	130	23·6	67	52	48

* No 195 was built with 19½in cylinders

LEADING DIMENSIONS
GREAT CENTRAL—SUPERHEATED ENGINES

Class		Cylinders			Driving Wheels	Working Pressure	Heating Surface			Grate Area	Weight		
GC	LNER	No	Dia	Stroke	Diameter	lb/sq/in	Tubes	Fire-box	Super-heater	sq ft	Engine	Ad-hesion	Tender
8	B5	2	19in	26in	6ft 1in	180	1280	145	220	23·6	63	48	48
8C	B1	2	19¼in	26in	6ft 9in	180	1349	154	242	26·3	67·6	52·5	48
8F	B4	2	21in	26in	6ft 7in	180	1349	154	242	26·3	70·7	54·9	48
8G	B9	2	19in	26in	5ft 3in	180	1280	145	220	23·6	67·3	52·1	48
1	B2	2	*21¼in	26in	6ft 9in	180	1881	163	343	26·0	75	57½	48
1A	B8	2	*21¼in	26in	5ft 7in	180	1881	163	343	26·0	74	56½	48
9P	B3	4	16in	26in	6ft 9in	180	1881	163	343	26·0	79	57	48
8N	B6	2	21in	26in	5ft 8in	180	1641	174	308	26·3	72	54	48
9Q	B7	4	16in	26in	5ft 8in	180	1881	163	343	26·0	79½	58½	48

*B2/2, B8/2, 20in cylinders

LEADING DIMENSIONS
GREAT EASTERN

Class	Cylinders			Driving Wheels	Working Pressure	Heating Surface sq ft			Grate Area	Weight		
	No	Dia	Stroke	Diameter	lb/sq/in	Tubes	Fire-box	Super-heater	sq ft	Engine	Ad-hesion	Tender
B12	2	20in	28in	6ft 6in	180	*1465	144	†202	26·5	64	44	39
B12/3	2	20in	28in	6ft 6in	180	1405	154	315	31·5	69	48	39
B12/4	2	20in	28in	6ft 6in	180	1355	143	202	26·5	63	43	39

* LNER figure, as originally built tube heating surface 1489sq ft. † Schmidt superheater with 286sq ft heating surface on first batch.

LNER

Class	Cylinders			Driving Wheels	Working Pressure	Heating Surface sq ft			Grate Area	Weight		
	No	Dia	Stroke	Diameter	lb/sq/in	Tubes	Fire-box	Super-heater	sq ft	Engine	Ad-hesion	Tender
B17	3	17½in	26in	6ft 8in	200*	1508	168	344	27·5	77	54	52½
B1	2	20in	26in	6ft 2in	225	1493	168	344	27·9	71	53	52½
B2	2	20in	26in	6ft 8in	225	1493	168	344	27·9	73·6	55	52½

Some B17 class engines originally had GER type 39 ton tenders.
* Some B17 class engines were reduced to 180 lb B.P. in 1943.
* Class B17/6 later had 225 lb B.P.

2 VALVES AND VALVE DIMENSIONS

A relatively small addition to the travel of the valves and a smaller addition to the lap of the valves have been known to transform the efficiency of a steam locomotive. Leaking piston valves have been known to increase coal consumption by 85 per cent before an engine has run its mileage before shopping. The valve design was one of the most important factors influencing performance.

Apart from the early GCR saturated engines and the first three NER Class S engines, which had flat valves, all the LNER 4–6–0s had piston valves. Piston valves could be either inside or outside admission. The NER used outside admission, the GER inside admission and the GCR rang the changes. The 4cyl GCR engines had outside admission to the outside cylinders with inside admission for the inside pair. This was done so that both sets of valves on each side of the engine could be worked from a common rocker worked by the inside valve gear. Outside admission valves had a tendency to leak at the valve spindles which were exposed to high pressure steam. In their later run down days the 4cyl GCR 4–6–0s were characterised by a high pressure wheeze.

The piston valves used on LNER 4–6–0s in pre grouping days tended to suffer from the contemporary defects of high wear and consequent steam leakage and from poor valve events due to short lap and short travel. Most contemporary locomotives on lines other than the GWR shared this deficiency. Exhaust clearance or negative lead was necessary and various pressure release features were usually incorporated in the valve heads to relieve the high compression pressures resulting from short laps and to provide release for trapped water.

On the NER the Worsdell engines had the Smith's patent segmented piston valves with spring loaded collapsing rings. The Raven engines used the simple Schmidt type broad ring valves without pressure relief features but with water relief valves in the cylinder covers.

The NER valves were $8\frac{3}{4}$in in diameter with steam lap $1\frac{1}{8}$in.

The GCR used the Robinson piston valves with a spring loaded disc valve and a single broad ring. The 2cyl engines had 10in valves with 1in lap and the 4cyl engines had 8in valves. The GCR piston valves were of the short "bobbin" type which needed long steam passages which was not a good feature.

The GER used 10in diameter valves with $1\frac{1}{8}$in lap.

The LNER used long lap, long travel valves after their value had been demonstrated by the GWR "Castle" in 1925.

The B17s had 8in diameter valves and the B1s had 10in valves both with $1\frac{5}{8}$in lap. Line on line exhaust setting was provided with no need for exhaust clearance. The B16 rebuilds had 9in valves with $1\frac{5}{8}$in lap.

From about 1926 onwards Gresley gradually introduced the narrow ring type valves, sometimes known as the Knorr ring type, with four rings per valve head. These made a dramatic improvement in steam tightness to the extent that it might be asked why they were not introduced earlier, as they were normal practice for the main cylinder pistons. On the LMS the introduction of narrow ring valves was vindicated by published test results but at first on the LNER there was some confusion about the correct method of valve setting. The early practice was to set to the valve head edge as was the previous practice, instead of to the valve ring which was the correct steam edge. This led to disappointing results and many drivers on NER and GCR engines, were and still are in some cases, convinced that Gresley had ruined their engines. The valve heads were later turned down before the rings and instructions given to ensure that the valves were set to the rings.

Nevertheless, when carboned up with poor maintenance the narrow ring valve tended to suffer from woolly valve events. In fairness to the old type valves they always provided a sharp cut off edge to set to, a quality that was shared by the Swindon semi-plug valve. The sharp exhaust crack of the GWR engines was due to this feature. In BR days a GWR engine was fitted with valves set to the ring in the LNER manner and the verdict was that it was a failure against which it could be claimed that there was plenty of good work done by such valves on the LNER. It would seem that, if steam had survived, more work on the development of valves would have been an advantage. In France Chapelon used an "L" shaped narrow ring, which gave good sealing whilst providing a sharp steam edge.

3 LIVERIES
NER
The passenger engines were finished in Saxony Green with black and white lining. They had large cast numberplates on the cab sides and the words NORTH EASTERN on the tender sides.

The goods engines were black with red lining, with a small cast number plate on the cab sides. The tender had large numerals flanked by the letters NE.

GCR
The passenger engines were finished in Brunswick green with red, white and black lining. In some cases the driving wheel splashers were claret. Large cast number plates were fixed to the cab sides and the words GREAT CENTRAL appeared on the tender. In the case of some large-wheeled 4–6–0s, which were clearly express passenger engines, goods black was used. GCR goods engines

were black with red lining. The large cast number-plates were on the cab sides, with the words GREAT CENTRAL on the tender.

GER

The 1500 class 4–6–0s were originally royal blue with black panelling, red lines, red coupling rods and brass beading. Oval number plates were on the cab sides and the letters GER on the tender.

During World War I the colour was changed to shop grey. Nos 1541–61 were delivered in grey with black panelling and red lines.

LNER

In 1924 GNR green was chosen, but the lining was not GNR style as the olive green edging was abandoned. Lining was black and white. At first the letters L&NER were placed on the tender sides in shaded lettering with the number underneath in larger figures. Later it was changed to LNER.

At first the original numbering was left unchanged, with letters added: D for NER; E for GER; and C for GCR. Later NER numbers were left unchanged; 5000 was added to all GCR and 7000 to all GER numbers.

A number of 4–6–0 classes were chosen for green livery; at first these were B1 (GCR), B2 (GCR), B3, B4, B12, and B14. The B13 engine No 2006 was painted green for the 1925 Darlington Centenary Procession.

In 1928 changes were made; it was desirable that engines should change tenders occasionally, notably the corridor tenders for the Edinburgh non-stop. The numbers were moved to the cab sides, leaving the letters LNER alone on the tender sides; letters and numbers were shaded. As an economy measure the number of green engines was reduced.

The LNER 4–6–0s remaining green were Classes B1 (GCR), B2 (GCR), B3, B4, B12 and the newly introduced B17.

The remaining LNER 4–6–0s were black with red lines.

World War

LNER engines were painted unlined black with the letters NE on the tender.

1946

The original intention was to paint all LNER engines green but with unshaded lettering. Only a few representative examples were completed before BR took over, but a considerable number of B1s were turned out in green before BR black was substituted. LNER classes of 4–6–0 with green representatives were:—

B1 (Standard), B2 (Standard), B3, B4, B12 and B17.

BR

There was a transitional period when the letters BRITISH RAILWAYS appeared on the tenders; later this was replaced by the BR emblem.

BR colours for LNER 4-6-os were:—

Brunswick green: B2 (Standard), B17.

LNWR-style lined black: B1 (Standard), B12, B16.

The remainder were left as they were until scrapping.

Class	Pre-Grouping	World War I	LNER	World War II	LNER (1946)	BR
B1 (Standard)				Black	Green	Black
B2 (Standard)					Green	Green
B3	GCR Green		Green	Black	Black or Green	
B4	GCR Green or Black		Green	Black	Black or Green	
B5	GCR Black		Black	Black	Black	
B6	GCR Black		Black	Black	Black	
B7	GCR Black		Black	Black	Black	
B8	GCR Black		Black	Black	Black	
B9	GCR Black		Black	Black	Black	
B12	GER Blue	Shop Grey	Green	Black	Black or Green	Black
B13	NER Green	Black	Black			
B14	NER Green	Black	Green			
B15	NER Green	Black	Black	Black	Black	
B16	NER Black	Black	Black	Black	Black	Black
B17			Green	Black	Black or Green	Green
B18 (B1)	GCR Green or Black		Green	Black	Black	
B19 (B2)	GCR Green or Black		Green	Black	Black	

4 ENGINE SUMMARY

LNER Class B

Original classification for B1 until 4/43.

LNER Class B1 (original)

GCR Class 8C 6ft 9in outside-cylinder express locomotive designed by J. G. Robinson. First engine built 12/03, last engine withdrawn 12/47. Reclassified B18, 4/43.

LNER Class B1

Thompson standard general purpose type. First engine built 12/42; last engine withdrawn 9/67.

LNER Class B2 (original)

GCR Class 1. "Sir Sam Fay" Class. Designed by J. G. Robinson. First engine built 12/12, last engine withdrawn 11/47. Reclassified Class B19, 8/45.

Subsections:

B2/1   21½in cylinders.

B2/2   20in cylinders.

LNER Class B2
Thompson, two-cylinder rebuild of Class B17. First engine rebuilt 8/45; last engine withdrawn 12/59.

LNER Class B3
GCR Class 9P 6ft 9in 4cyl express locomotives. Designed by J. G. Robinson. First engine built 11/17; last engine withdrawn 12/47.
Subsections:
B3/1   4cyl. Stephensons gear, piston valves.
B3/2   4cyl. Caprotti valve gears.
B3/3   Complete rebuild by Thompson of No 6166 to two cylinders with 225 lb boiler. Withdrawn 4/49.

LNER Class B4
GCR Class 8F, "Immingham" class; as Class 8C but 6ft 7in wheels Designed by J. G. Robinson. First engine built 5/06; last engine withdrawn 11/50.
Subsections:
B4/1 (original) Saturated slide valve engines.
B4/1 (later)   Superheated, 21in cyls., piston valves.
B4/2   Original cyls, but superheated.
B4/3   Piston valves, 21in cyls, reduced to LNER loading gauge.
B4/4   Slide valves, 19in cyls, reduced to LNER loading gauge.

LNER Class B5
GCR Class 8 "Fish Engines"; 6ft 1in mixed traffic engines. Designed by J. G. Robinson. First engine built 11/02; last engine withdrawn 6/50.
Subsections:
B5/1   Original saturated engines.
B5/2   Rebuild with larger superheated boiler.
B5/3   Superheated, reduced to LNER loading gauge.

LNER Class B6
GCR Class 8N, 2cyl, 5ft 8in mixed traffic engines. Designed by J. G. Robinson. First engine built 7/18; last engine withdrawn 12/47.

LNER B7
GCR 9Q 4cyl, 5ft 8in mixed traffic engines. Designed by J. G. Robinson. First engine built 5/21; last engine withdrawn 7/50.
Subsections:
B7/1   GCR loading gauge.
B7/2   LNER loading gauge.

LNER Class B8
GCR Class 1A, inside cylinder 5ft 7in wheeled "Glenalmond"

class. Designed by J. G. Robinson. First engine built 6/13; last engine withdrawn 4/49.
Subsections:
B8/1   21½in cylinders.
B8/2   20in cylinders.

LNER Class B9
GCR Class 8G, 5ft 3in 2cyl freight engines. Designed by J. G. Robinson. First engine built 9/06; last engine withdrawn 5/49.
Subsections:
B9/1   retaining saturated boiler.
B9/2   superheated, higher pitched boiler.

LNER Class B12
GER S.D. Holden express engines. First engine built 12/11; last engine withdrawn 11/54.
Subsections:
B12/1   original (more usually called B12).
B12/2   Lentz poppet valves.
B12/3   Gresley rebuild with larger round top boiler and modernised valve motion.
B12/4   Rebuilt, Thompson, with small round top boiler for GNSR.

LNER Class B13
NER Class S. W. Worsdell mixed traffic engines. First engine built 6/99; last engine withdrawn 5/51.

LNER Class B14
NER Class S1. W. Worsdell express engines. First engine built 12/1900; last engine withdrawn 4/31.

LNER Class B15
NER Class S2. V. Raven 2cyl mixed traffic engines. First engine built 12/11; last engine withdrawn 12/47.

LNER Class B16
NER Class S3. V. Raven 3cyl mixed traffic engines. First engine built 12/1900; last engine withdrawn 11/64.
Subsections:
B16/1   Original Raven design with Stephenson's gear.
B16/2   Gresley rebuilds with 2-and-1 gear.
B16/3   Thompson rebuilds with separate sets of Walschaert gear.

LNER Class B17
Gresley/North British Loco Co. "Sandringham" class. First engine built 12/28; last engine withdrawn 8/60.
Subsections:
B17/1   As originally built, short tender. Original Classes B17/1/2/3

with different springs all combined with 15 plate springs in B17/1.

B17/4   Engines with 4200 gallon tender.
B17/5   Streamlined version.
B17/6   With 225 lb boiler.

LNER Class B18
Former B1, GCR 8C, reclassified to make room for standard B1.

LNER Class B19
Former B2, GCR 1, reclassified to make room for standard B2.
Subsections:
B19/1   former B2/1.
B19/2   former B2/2.

5 RUNNING NUMBERS

Class	Pre-grouping Nos	LNER (post 1924) Nos	LNER (post 1946) Nos
B1 (later B18) GCR	195/6	5195/6	1479/80
B2 (later B19) GCR	423–8	5423–8	1490–3
B3 GCR	1164–9	6164–9	1494–9
B4 GCR	1095–1104	6095–6104	1481–9
B5 GCR	180–7 1067–72	5180–7 6067–72	1678–90
B6 GCR	52/3 416	5052/3 5416	1346/7/8
B7 GCR	31–8 72/3/8 58–74	5031–8 5072/3/4 5458–74 (built 1923–24) 5475–5484	1360–97; renumbered in 1949; 61702–7/ 9–13
B8 GCR	4, 279/80 439–46	5004, 5279/80 5439–46	1349–59
B9 GCR	1105–14	6105–14	1469–78
B12 GER	1500–1580 (1506 scrapped 1913)	8500–8580 (8506 blank)	1500–80 (1506 blank)
B13 NER	726, 738–41/3–63/ 6/8/75 1077,2001–10	Unchanged	1699
B14 NER	2111–5	Unchanged (extinct 1931)	
B15 NER	782/6/7/8/91/5–9 813/5/7/9–25	Unchanged	1313–27; Renumbered in 1949; 1691–8
B16 NER	840–9, 906/8/9/11/ 4/5/20–34/6/7/42/3 2363/4/5	Unchanged built 1923/4 2366–82 1371–85	1400–1468; in 1949 Nos 61400–9 became 61469–78 after extinction of Class B9
B17 LNER		2800–2872	1600–1672
B1 LNER		8301–8310	1000–1009 1010–1273 61274–61409 (BR)

Re-numbering policy

1

1924, NER left unchanged, 5000 added to GCR, 7000 added to GER.

2

Nationalisation. At first the prefix 'E' was added to LNER engine numbers. From March, 1948 onwards 60000 added to LNER engine numbers.

3

The original LNER re-numbering scheme of 1943, implemented in 1946, intended numbers 1000–1299 for B1 class engines. When more were built some GCR and NER classes numbered over 1300 were re-numbered as shown above. Some had been scrapped before this was carried out, but some engines carried the original numbers for a short time.

4

1943 intention, not implemented except for B7s:

B3	1480–5	B8	1331–41
B4	1490–9	B9	1342–51
B5	1300–12	B15	1313–27
B6	1328–30	B18	1470–1
B7	1360–1397	B19	1472–7

When B1s 61360–61409 were built in 1949–52 there was certain re-numbering of engines which had carried numbers in this range for some years.

6 LOADING CLASSIFICATION

LNER, SOUTHERN AREA (FREIGHT)

Load class 6	B7, B16
Load class 5	B1 (standard), B6, B8
Load class 4	B2 (standard), B3, B17
Load class 3	B9, B12, B13, B15
Load class 2	B1 (GCR), B2 (GCR), B4, B5

BR POWER CLASSIFICATION 1949

Power class 6	B16, B7 (MT)
Power class 5	B1, B8, B9 (MT), B17/6 (Passenger)
Power class 4	B2, B3, B4, B12, B17 (passenger)
Power class 3	B5 (MT)

BR POWER CLASSIFICATION 1953

Power class 6	B16/2, B16/3
Power class 5	B1, B16/1 (MT), B2, B17/6 (passenger)
Power class 4	B12, B17 (passenger).

LOAD LIMITS Class 5 engines.

	Bı class	
	Full load	*Limited load*
Marylebone–Woodford		
via Aylesbury	345 tons	310 tons
via High Wycombe	370 tons	335 tons
Woodford–Nottingham	370 tons	335 tons
Nottingham–Pilsey	355 tons	310 tons
West Highland Line	255 tons	

7 TENDERS

North Eastern	Class B16	5½ tons coal	4125 gallons water
	Class B13/14/15	5 tons coal	3940 gallons water
Great Central	All 4–6–0s	6 tons coal	4000 gallons water
Great Eastern	B12s	4 tons coal	3700 gallons water
LNER	B17	4 tons coal	3700 gallons water
	B17/4	7½ tons coal	4200 gallons water
	B1	7½ tons coal	4200 gallons water

Two B2 class engines, rebuilds from Class B17, had tenders from the P2 class 2–8–2s when those engines were scrapped. Seven B2s had NER tenders from C7s. Four self-weighing tenders ran at times with various B1 class engines. Some B17s which originally had the GER type tender later had Group Standard tenders as with Class B17/4.

8 NAMES AND NUMBERS

B1 Class (standard)

1000	*Springbok*	1018	*Gnu*
1001	*Eland*	1019	*Nilghai*
1002	*Impala*	1020	*Gemsbok*
1003	*Gazelle*	1021	*Reitbok*
1004	*Oryx*	1022	*Sassaby*
1005	*Bongo*	1023	*Hirola*
1006	*Blackbuck*	1024	*Addax*
1007	*Klipspringer*	1025	*Pallah*
1008	*Kudu*	1026	*Ourebi*
1009	*Hartebeeste*	1027	*Madoqua*
1010	*Wildebeeste*	1028	*Umseke*
1011	*Waterbuck*	1029	*Chamois*
1012	*Puku*	1030	*Nyala*
1013	*Topi*	1031	*Reedbuck*
1014	*Oribi*	1032	*Stembok*
1015	*Duiker*	1033	*Dibatag*
1016	*Inyala*	1034	*Chiru*
1017	*Bushbuck*	1035	*Pronghorn*

1036	Ralph Assheton	1242	Alexander Reith Gray
1037	Jairou	1243	Sir Harold Mitchell
1038	Blacktail	1244	Strang Steel
1039	Steinbok	1245	Murray of Elibank
1040	Roedeer	1246	Lord Balfour of Burleigh
1189	Sir William Gray	1247	Lord Burghley
1215	William Henton Carver	1248	Geoffrey Gibbs
1221	Sir Alexander Erskine-Hill	1249	Fitzherbert Wright
1237	Geoffrey H. Kitson	1250	A. Harold Bibby
1238	Leslie Runciman	1251	Oliver Bury
1240	Harry Hinchliffe	61379	Mayflower (7/51)
1241	Viscount Ridley		

Nos 1000–1009 originally Nos 8301–8310.
LNER re-numbering scheme introduced 1946.
60000 added to all LNER engines after nationalisation.

B2 Class (GCR) later Class B19

5423	1490	Sir Sam Fay	5426	—	City of Chester
5424	—	City of Lincoln	5427	1482	City of London
5425	1491	City of Manchester	5428	1493	City of Liverpool

No 5427 names removed 9/37, name used on streamlined B17.

B3 Class (GCR)

6169	1494	Lord Faringdon	6166	1496	Earl Haig
6164	1495	Earl Beatty	6167	1498	Lloyd George
6165	1496	Valour	6168	—	Lord Stuart of Wortley

Name removed from 6166 10/43 when rebuilt as Class B3/3.
Name removed from 6167 8/23 as a result of political unpopularity.

B4 Class (GCR)

6097	1482	Immingham

B8 Class (GCR)

5004	1349	Glenalmond	5446	1357	Earl Roberts of Kandahar
5439	1350	Sutton Nelthorpe	5279	1358	Earl Kitchener of Khartoum

B17 Class (LNER). Some rebuilt with 2 cylinders as Class B2.

2800	1600	Sandringham
2801	1601	Holkham
2802	1602	Walsingham
2803	1603	Framlingham rebuilt B2 10/46
2804	1604	Elveden
2805	1605	Burnham Thorpe renamed Lincolnshire Regiment 4/38

2806	1606	*Audley End*
2807	1607	*Blickling* rebuilt B2 5/47
2808	1608	*Gunton*
2809	1609	*Quidenham*
2810	1610	*Honingham Hall*
2811	1611	*Raynham Hall*
2812	1612	*Houghton Hall*
2813	1613	*Woodbastwick Hall*
2814	1614	*Castle Hedingham* rebuilt B2 11/46
2815	1615	*Culford Hall* rebuilt B2 9/46
2816	1616	*Fallodon* rebuilt B2 11/45
2817	1617	*Ford Castle* rebuilt 12/46
2818	1618	*Wynyard Park*
2819	1619	*Welbeck Abbey*
2820	1620	*Clumber*
2821	1621	*Hatfield House*
2822	1622	*Alnwick Castle*
2823	1623	*Lambton Castle*
2824	1624	*Lumley Castle*
2825	1625	*Raby Castle*
2826	1626	*Brancepeth Castle*
2827	1627	*Aske Hall*
2828	1628	*Harewood House*
2829	1629	*Naworth Castle*
2830	1630	*Thoresby Park* renamed *Tottenham Hotspur* 1/38
2831	1631	*Serlby Hall*
2832	1632	*Belvoir Castle* rebuilt B2 7/46: renamed *Royal Sovereign* 10/58
2833	1633	*Kimbolton Castle*
2834	1634	*Hinchingbrooke*
2835	1635	*Milton*
2836	1636	*Harlaxton Manor*
2837	1637	*Thorpe Hall*
2838	1638	*Melton Hall*
2839	1639	*Rendlesham Hall* renamed *Norwich City* 1/38: rebuilt B2 1/46
2840	1640	*Somerleyton Hall*
2841	1641	*Gayton Hall*
2842	1642	*Kilverstone Hall*
2843	1643	*Champion Lodge*
2844	1644	*Earlham Hall* rebuilt B2 3/49
2845	1645	*The Suffolk Regiment*
2846	1646	*Gilwell Park*
2847	1647	*Helmingham Hall*
2848	1648	*Arsenal*
2849	1649	*Sheffield United*

2850	1650	*Grimsby Town*
2851	1651	*Derby County*
2852	1652	*Darlington*
2853	1653	*Huddersfield Town*
2854	1654	*Sunderland*
2855	1655	*Middlesbrough*
2856	1656	*Leeds United*
2857	1657	*Doncaster Rovers*
2858	1658	*Newcastle United* renamed *The Essex Regiment* 6/36
2859	1659	*Norwich City* renamed *East Anglian* and streamlined 9/37
2860	1660	*Hull City*
2861	1661	*Sheffield Wednesday*
2862	1662	*Manchester United*
2863	1663	*Everton*
2864	1664	*Liverpool*
2865	1665	*Leicester City*
2866	1666	*Nottingham Forest*
2867	1667	*Bradford*
2868	1668	*Bradford City*
2869	1669	*Barnsley*
2870	1670	*Manchester City* renamed *Tottenham Hotspur* 5/37: renamed *City of London* and streamlined 9/37
2871	1671	*Manchester City* rebuilt B2 6/45: renamed *Royal Sovereign* 4/46
2872	1672	*West Ham United*

A number of one-day only changes of nameplates took place with the Football Club engines when called out to work supporters' specials.

9 Nameplates

B1   Straight nameplates on smoke box sides.

B2/B19 Straight nameplates below upper edge of continuous splasher.

B2   Curved nameplate over middle splasher as in B17 class.

B3   Straight nameplate under upper edge of continuous splasher.

No 6165 *Valour*, War Memorial nameplate inscribed:

In memory of

GCR Employees

who gave their lives for their country

1914–1918

B4 Originally curved nameplate above centre splasher later changed to a smaller plate below upper edge of centre splasher.

B8 Straight nameplate above upper edge of continuous splasher.

B17 Curved nameplates above centre splasher.
Football Club series had a raised metal impression of a football flanked by the club colours on the centre splasher. The two streamlined engines had straight nameplates on outer casing at the smokebox end.

10 Class Totals

	Engines		Engines
B1 Standard	410	B8	11
B1 (GCR) B18	2	B9	10
B2 (GCR) B19	6	B12	80
B3	6	B13	40
B4	10	B14	5
B5	14	B15	20
B6	3	B16	70
B7	38	B17	73

Major rebuilds

B3 rebuilt as B3/3	1
B16 rebuilt as B16/2	7
B16 rebuilt as B16/3	17
B17 rebuilt as B2	10

11 Building, B1 and B17 Classes

B17

2800–2809	1928	North British Loco Co (Hyde Park Works)
2810–2821	1930	Darlington Works
2822–2836	1931	Darlington Works
2837–2842	1933	Darlington Works
2843–2847	1935	Darlington Works
2848–2861	1936	Darlington Works
2862–2872	1937	R. Stephenson & Co

B1

8301 (1000)	1942	Darlington Works
8302–5 (1001-4)	1943	Darlington Works
8306–10 (1005-9)	1944	Darlington Works
1010–1014	1946	Darlington Works
1040–1112	1946	North British Loco Co

1015–1039	1947	Darlington Works
1140–1189	1947	Vulcan Foundry
1113–1139	1947	North British Loco Co
1190–1273	1947	North British Loco Co
61274–61339	1948	North British Loco Co
61340/1	1948	Gorton Works
61342–61349	1949	Gorton Works
61350–61359	1949	Darlington Works
61360–61373	1950	North British Loco Co
61400–61409	1950	Darlington Works
61374–61392	1951	North British Loco Co
61393–61399	1952	North British Loco Co

12 PRESERVATION

B1 No 1306 is preserved at The Steam Railway Museum Carnforth with the name *Mayflower*, formerly carried by No 61379. It is painted LNER apple green but its LNER number was never carried in service. It was built as BR No 61306.

B12/3 No 8572 is preserved at Sheringham. It is painted in LNER apple green with its LNER number 8572 restored.

An appeal is being made for the restoration of B1 No 61264, in a South Wales scrapyard at the time of writing.

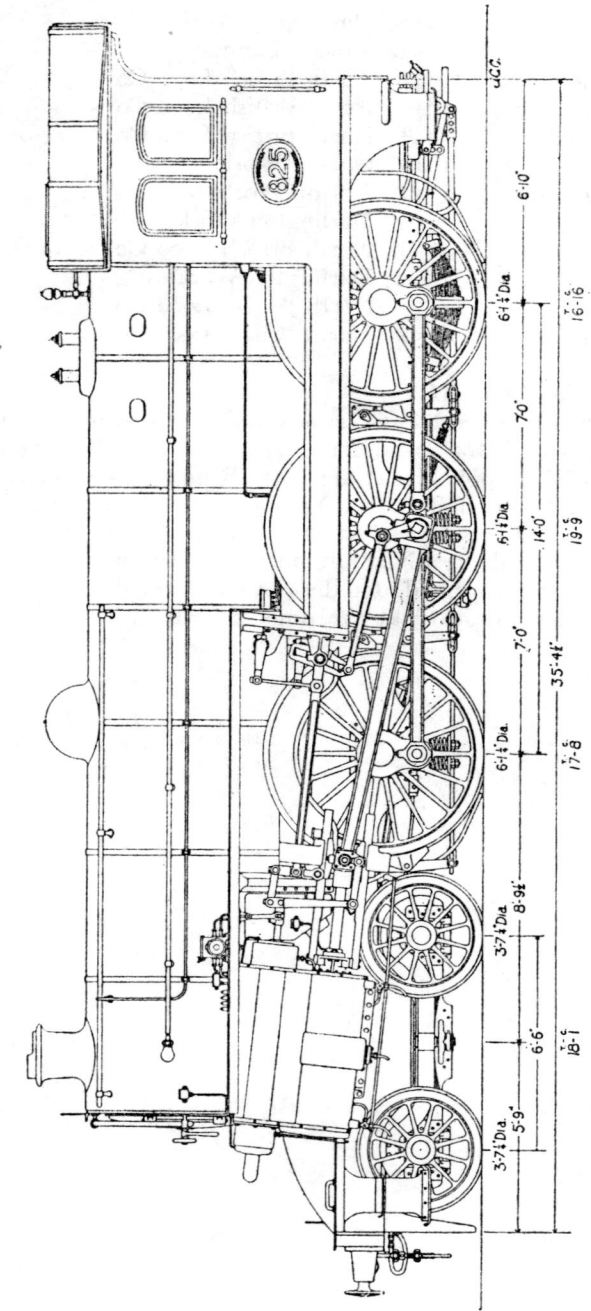

Class B15 No. 825 as built with Stumpf Uniflow Cylinders

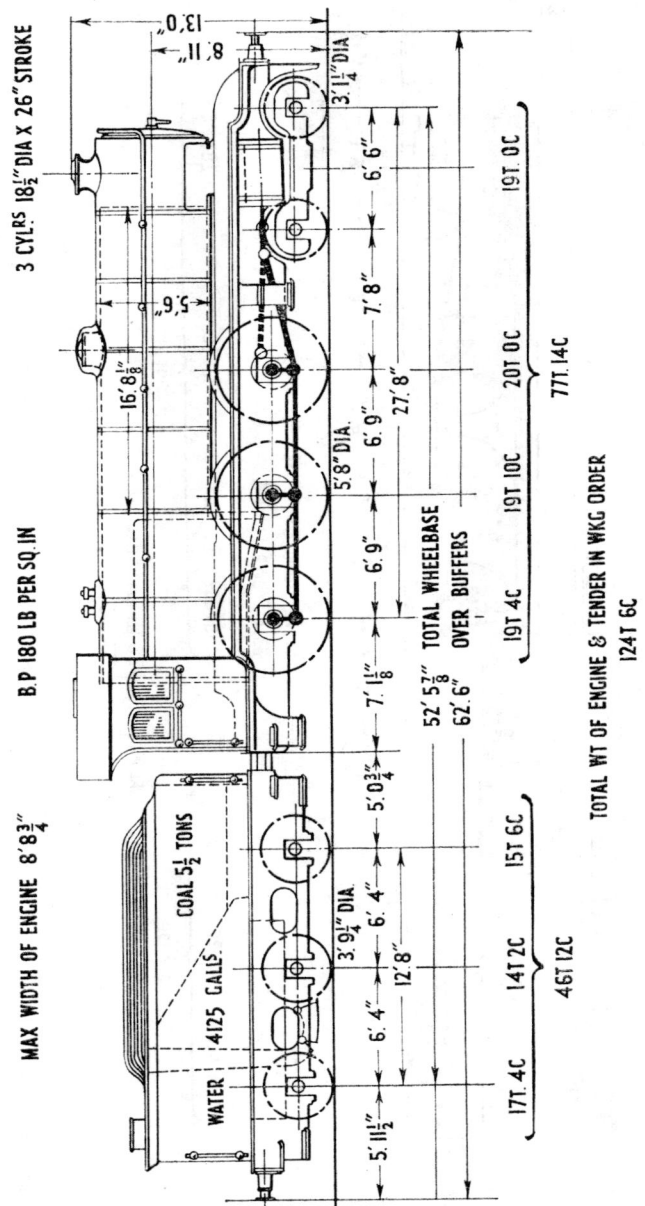

3 CYL.^RS 18½" DIA X 26" STROKE

B.P 180 LB PER SQ.IN

MAX WIDTH OF ENGINE 8'8¾"

COAL 5½ TONS

WATER 4125 GALLS.

TOTAL WHEELBASE OVER BUFFERS

TOTAL WT OF ENGINE & TENDER IN WKG ORDER
124T 6C

Class B16/1

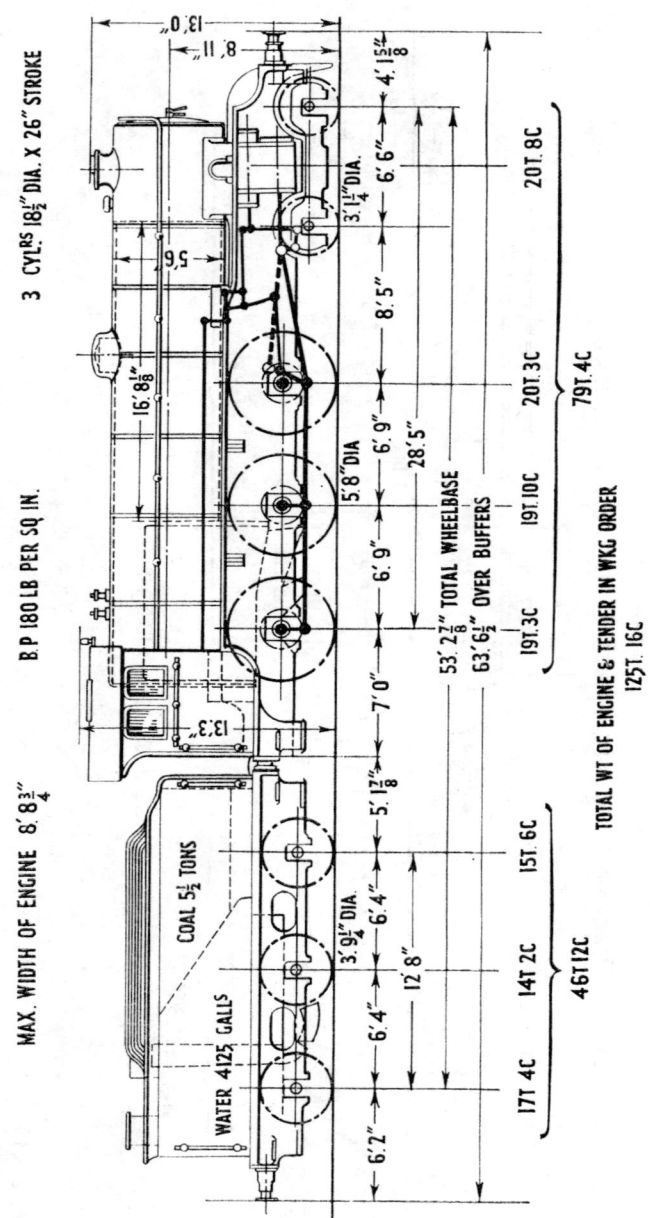

3 CYLRS 18½" DIA. X 26" STROKE

B.P 180 LB PER SQ IN.

MAX. WIDTH OF ENGINE 8' 8¾"

13' 0"

8' 11"

5' 6"

16' 8⅛"

13' 3"

4' 1⅝"

6' 6"   20T. 8C

3' 1¼" DIA.

8' 5"   20T. 3C   79T. 4C

6' 9"

5' 8" DIA   19T. 10C   28' 5"

53' 2⅞" TOTAL WHEELBASE
63' 6½" OVER BUFFERS

6' 9"   19T. 3C

7' 0"

5' 1⅛"   15T. 6C

COAL 5½ TONS

3' 9¼" DIA.

6' 4"   14T. 2C   46T12C

12' 8"

6' 4"   17T. 4C

WATER 4125 GALLS

6' 2"

TOTAL WT OF ENGINE & TENDER IN WKG ORDER
125T. 16C

Class B16/2

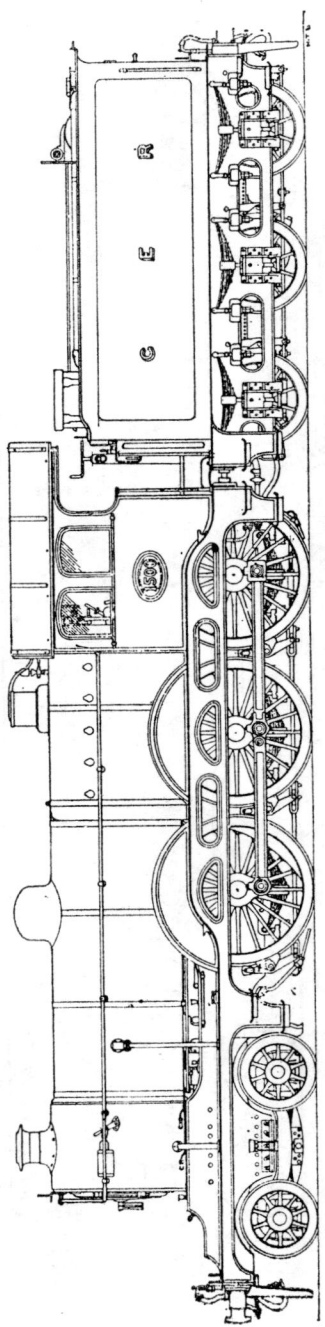

Class B12/1 as built

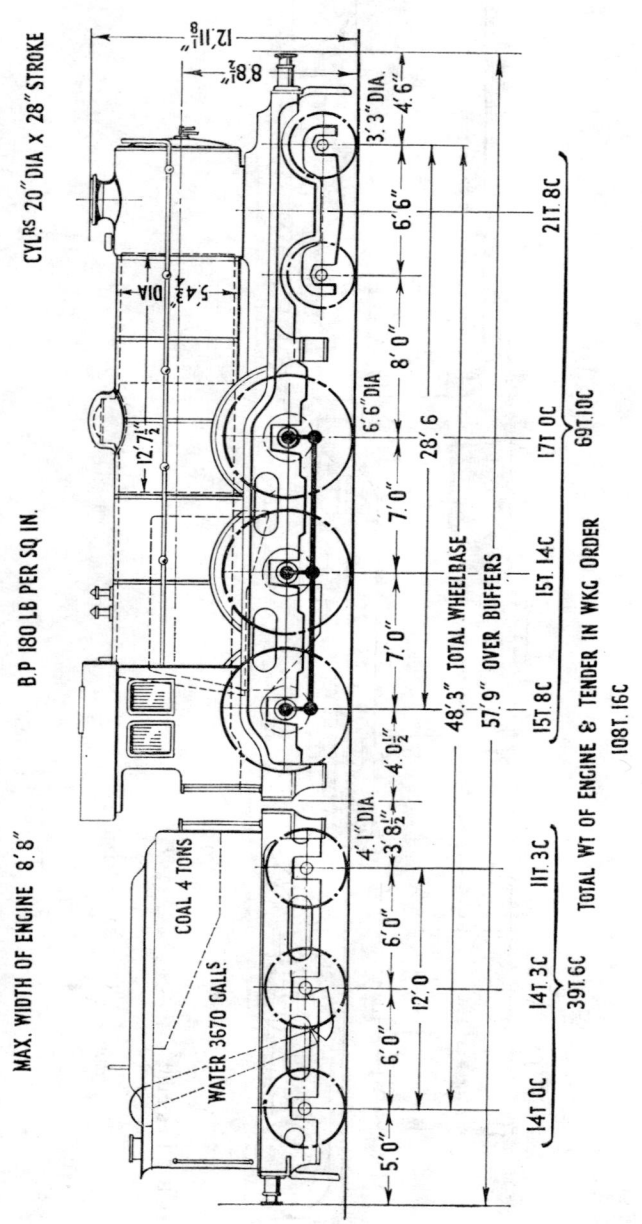

MAX. WIDTH OF ENGINE 8'8"

B.P 180 LB PER SQ IN.

CYL.RS 20" DIA x 28" STROKE

COAL 4 TONS

WATER 3670 GALLS.

5'4½" DIA

12'7½"

6'6" DIA.

3'3"DIA.

4'1" DIA.

12'11⅞"

8'8½"

4'6"

6'6"

8'0"

28'6

7'0"

7'0"

4'0½"

3'8½"

6'0"

12'0

6'0"

5'0"

48'3" TOTAL WHEELBASE

57'9" OVER BUFFERS

TOTAL WT OF ENGINE & TENDER IN WKG ORDER

14T 0C

14T 3C

11T 3C

15T 8C

15T 14C

17T 0C

21T 8C

39T.6C

69T.10C

108T.16C

Class B12/3

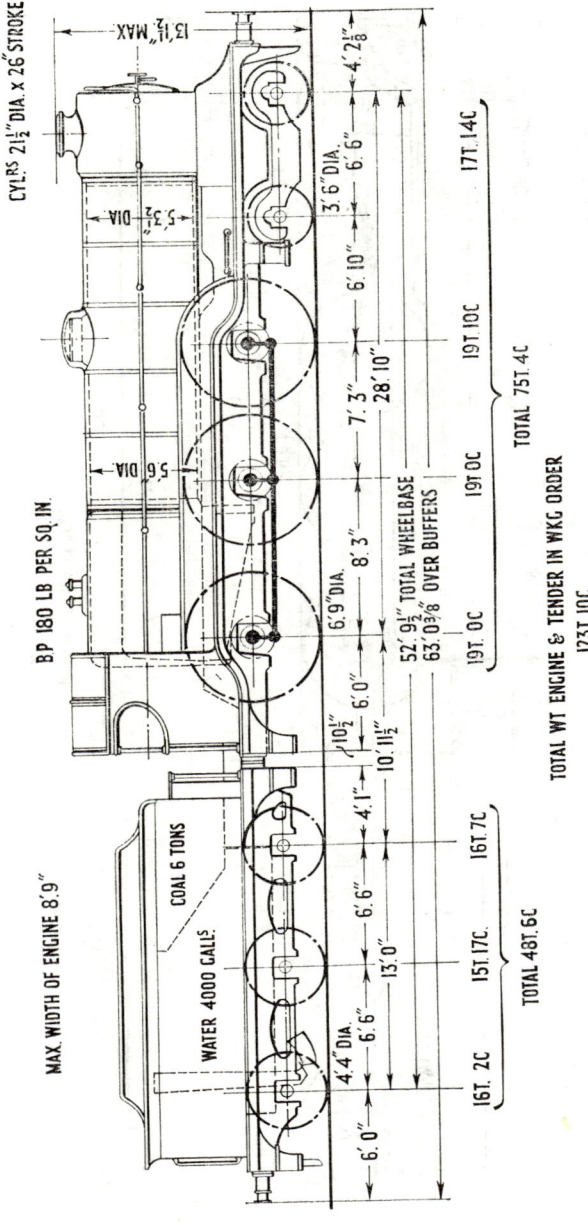

CYLRS 21½" DIA. x 26" STROKE

13' 1½" MAX.

5' 3½" DIA.

5' 6" DIA.

BP 180 LB PER SQ. IN.

MAX. WIDTH OF ENGINE 8' 9"

COAL 6 TONS

WATER 4000 GALLS.

3' 6" DIA.

4' 2⅛"

6' 6"

6' 10"

28' 10"

7' 3"

8' 3"

6' 9" DIA.

52' 9¼" TOTAL WHEELBASE

63' 0⅜" OVER BUFFERS

6' 0"

10' 1½"

10½"

4' 1"

6' 6"

13' 0"

4' 4" DIA.

6' 6"

6' 0"

17T. 14C.

19T. 10C.

19T. 0C.

19T. 0C.

TOTAL 75T. 4C.

16T. 7C.

15T. 17C.

16T. 2C.

TOTAL 48T. 6C.

TOTAL WT ENGINE & TENDER IN WKG ORDER
123T. 10C.

Class B2 (Ex-G.C.R.), Reclassified B19 in 1945

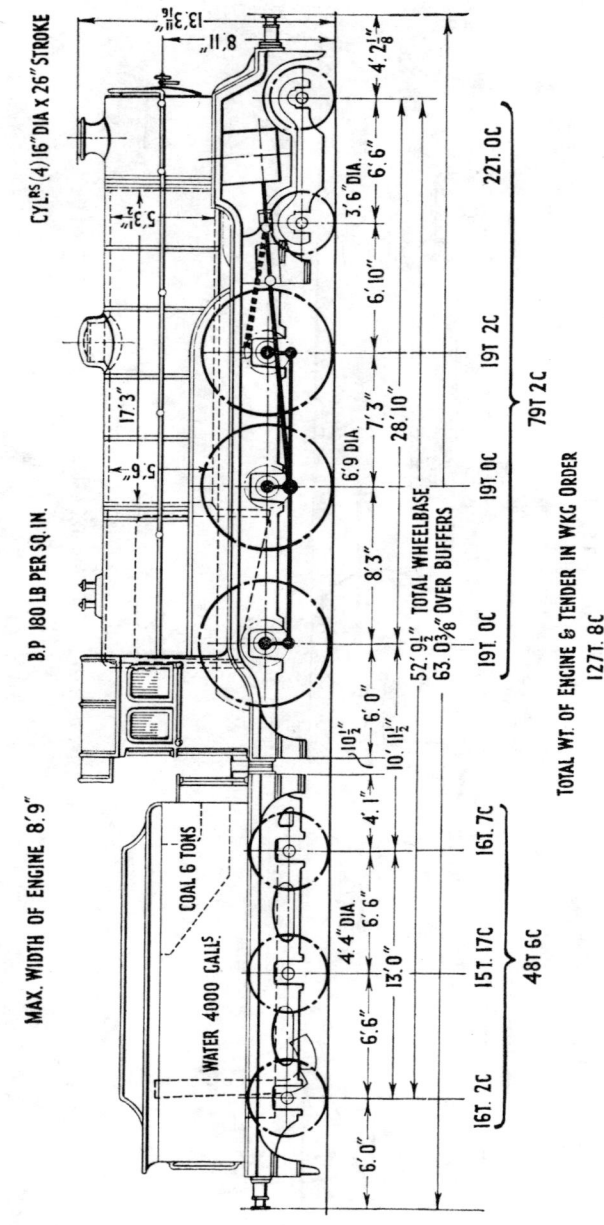

MAX. WIDTH OF ENGINE 8'9"

B.P 180 LB PER SQ. IN.

CYL.RS (4) 16" DIA x 26" STROKE

TOTAL WT. OF ENGINE & TENDER IN WKG ORDER
127T. 8C

Class B3/1

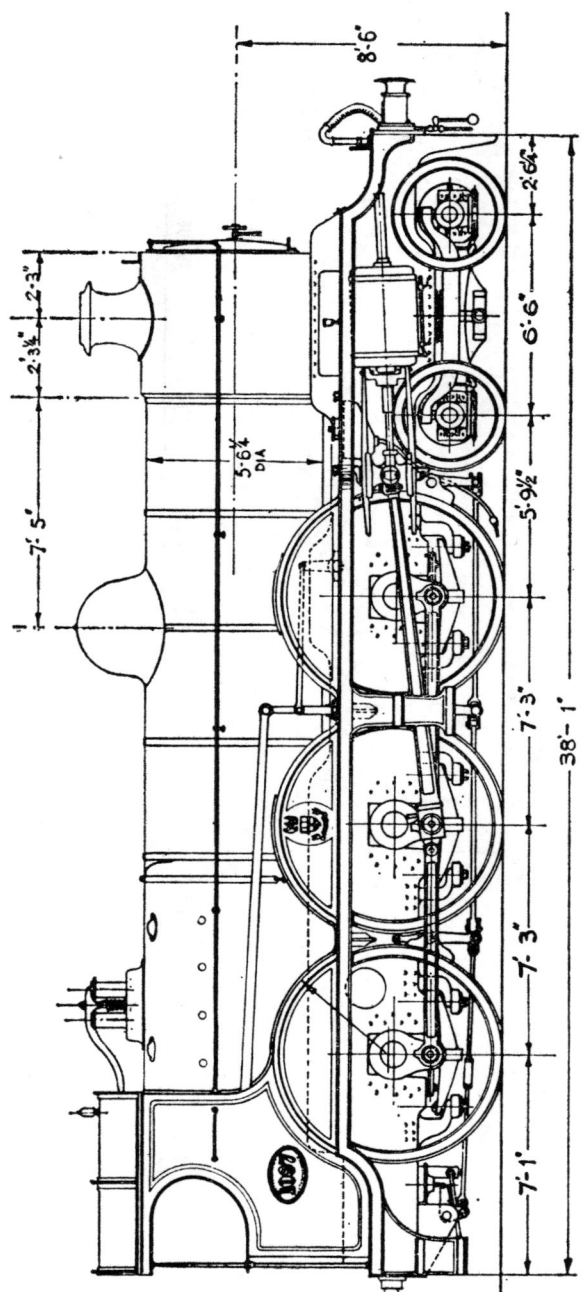

WHEELS DRIVING 6'·6" 21 SPOKES. BOGIE 3'·6" DIA. 10 SPOKES. CYLS 19½" DIA × 26" STROKE.

Class B4/1

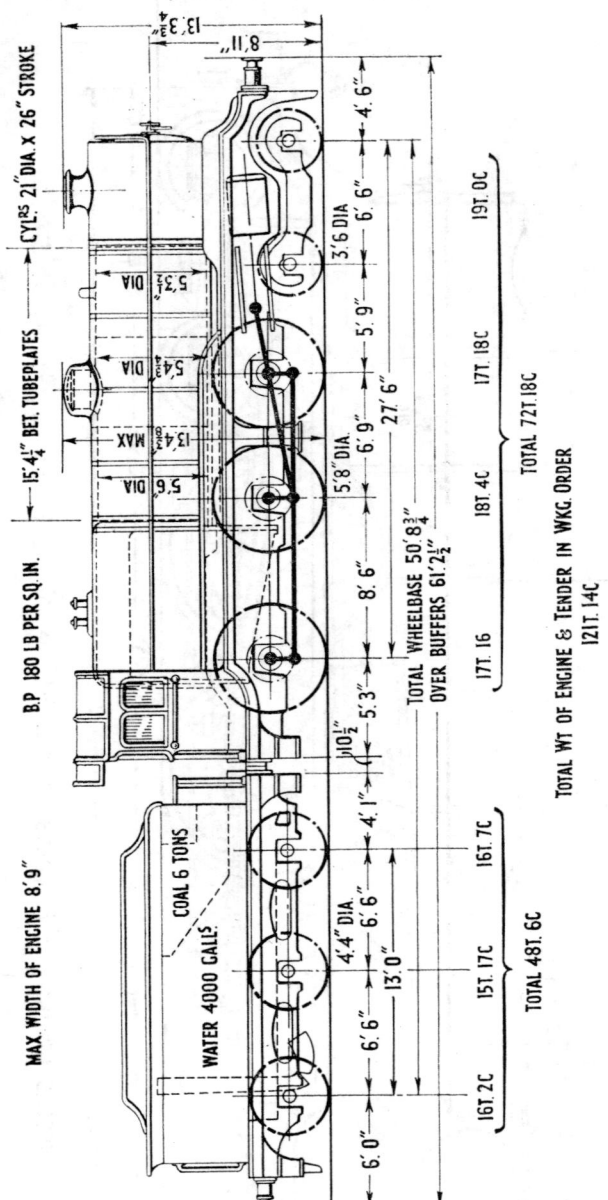

MAX WIDTH OF ENGINE 8'9"

B.P. 180 LB PER SQ.IN.

CYL.RS 21" DIA. X 26" STROKE

15'4¼" BET. TUBEPLATES

5'3½" DIA

5'4⅜" DIA

13'4⅜" MAX

5'6" DIA

COAL 6 TONS

WATER 4000 GALLS

13'3¾"

8'11"

4'6"

6'6"

3'6 DIA

5'9"

27'6"

6'9"

5'8" DIA

6'9"

8'6"

TOTAL WHEELBASE 50'8¾"
OVER BUFFERS 61'2½"

5'3"

10½"

4'1"

6'6"

4'4" DIA

13'0"

6'6"

6'0"

16T.2C   15T.17C   16T.7C   17T.16   18T.4C   17T.18C   19T.0C

TOTAL 48T.6C

TOTAL 72T.18C

TOTAL WT OF ENGINE & TENDER IN WKG. ORDER
121T.14C

Class B6

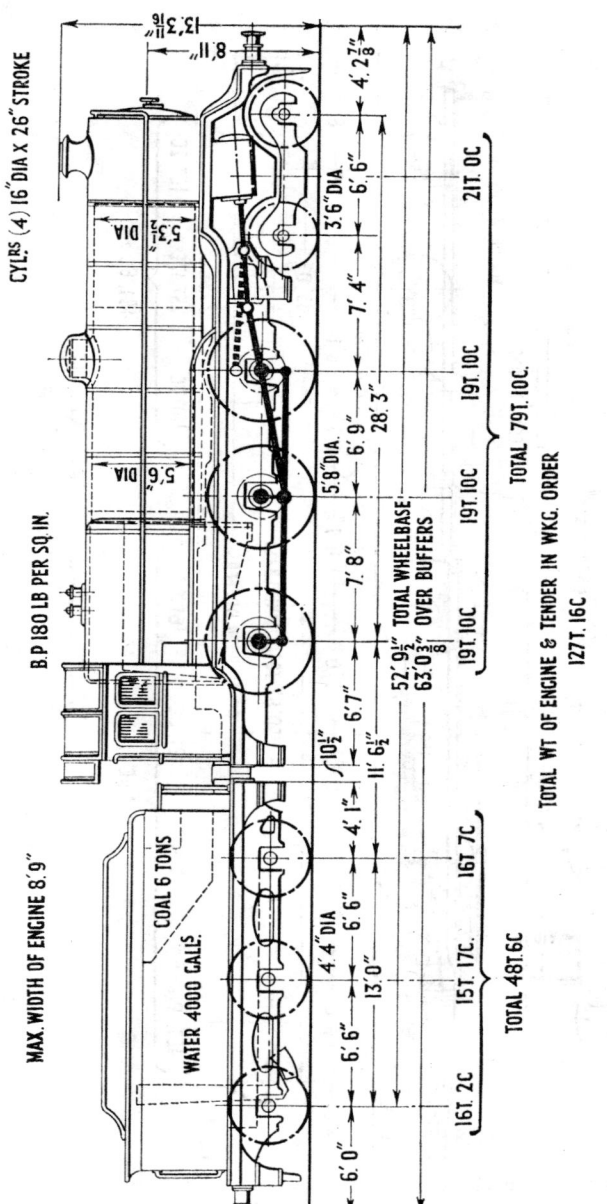

CYLRS (4) 16" DIA x 26" STROKE

B.P 180 LB PER SQ IN.

MAX. WIDTH OF ENGINE 8'9"

COAL 6 TONS

WATER 4000 GALLS

13'3 9/16"

8'11"

4' 2 7/8"

3'6"DIA.

6'6"

21T. 0C

5'3½" DIA

7'4"

5'6" DIA.

5'8"DIA.

28'3"

6'9"

19T. 10C

19T. 10C

19T. 10C

TOTAL 79T. 10C.

7'8"

TOTAL WHEELBASE

OVER BUFFERS

52'9½"

63'0⅜"

19T. 10C

6'7"

10½"

11'6½"

TOTAL WT OF ENGINE & TENDER IN WKG. ORDER

127T. 16C

4'1"

4'4 DIA

6'6"

16T 7C

13'0"

15T. 17C.

6'6"

16T. 2C

6'0"

TOTAL 48T.6C

Class B7/1

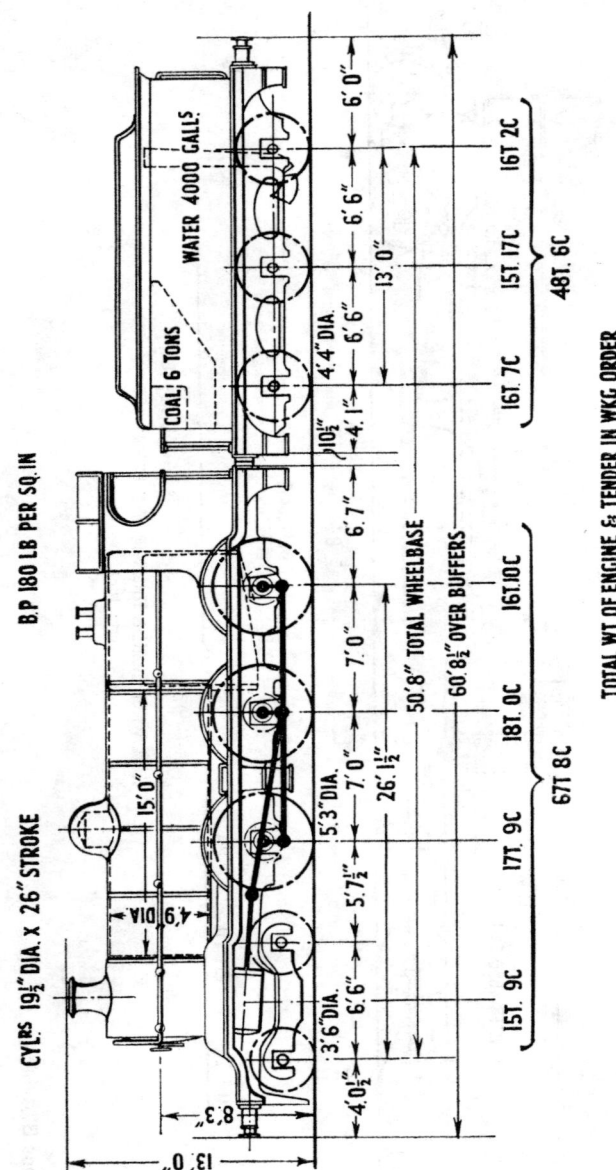

CYL^RS 19½" DIA. x 26" STROKE

B.P 180 LB PER SQ. IN

WATER 4000 GALL.S

COAL 6 TONS

TOTAL WT OF ENGINE & TENDER IN WKG ORDER
115T. 14C

Class B9/1

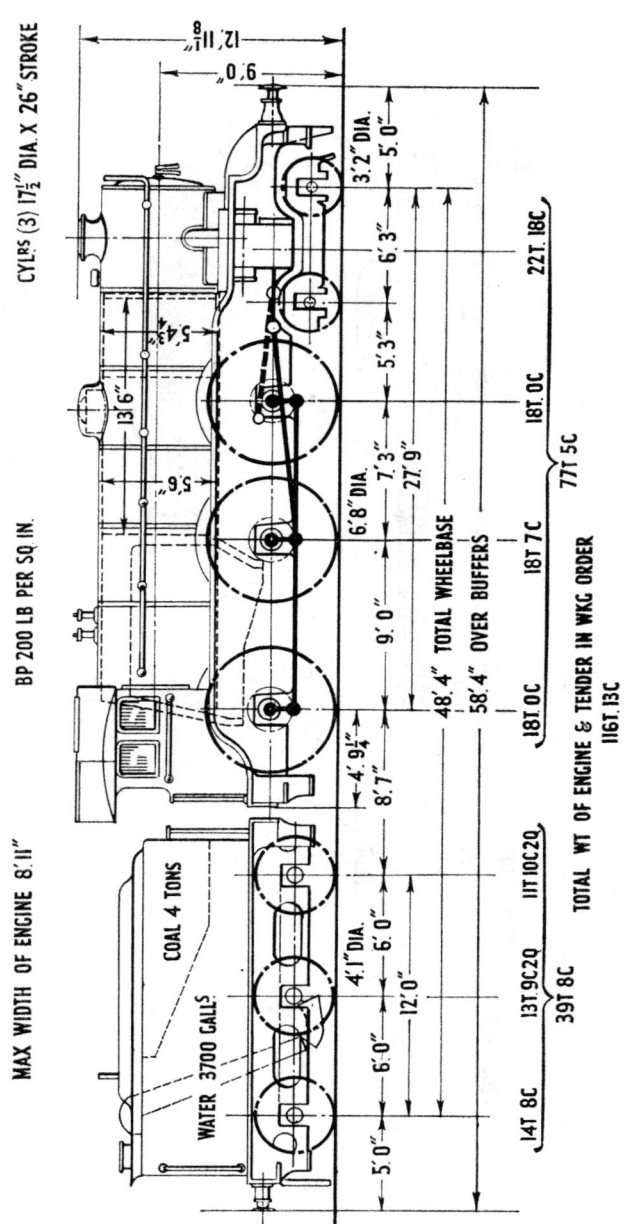

MAX WIDTH OF ENGINE 8'.II"

BP 200 LB PER SQ IN.

CYLRS (3) 17½" DIA. X 26" STROKE

12'.II⅛"

9'.0"

3'.2" DIA.

5'.0"

6'.3"

5'.4¾"

13'.6"

5'.3"

5'.6"

6'.8" DIA.

7'.3"

27'.9"

9'.0"

COAL 4 TONS

4'.9¼"

8'.7"

4'.I" DIA.

6'.0"

WATER 3700 GALLS

12'.0"

6'.0"

5'.0"

48'.4" TOTAL WHEELBASE

58'.4" OVER BUFFERS

22T. 18C

18T. 0C

77T. 5C

18T. 7C

18T. 0C

116T. 13C

TOTAL WT OF ENGINE & TENDER IN WKG ORDER

11T. 10C. 2Q

13T. 9C. 2Q

39T. 8C

14T. 8C

Class B17/1

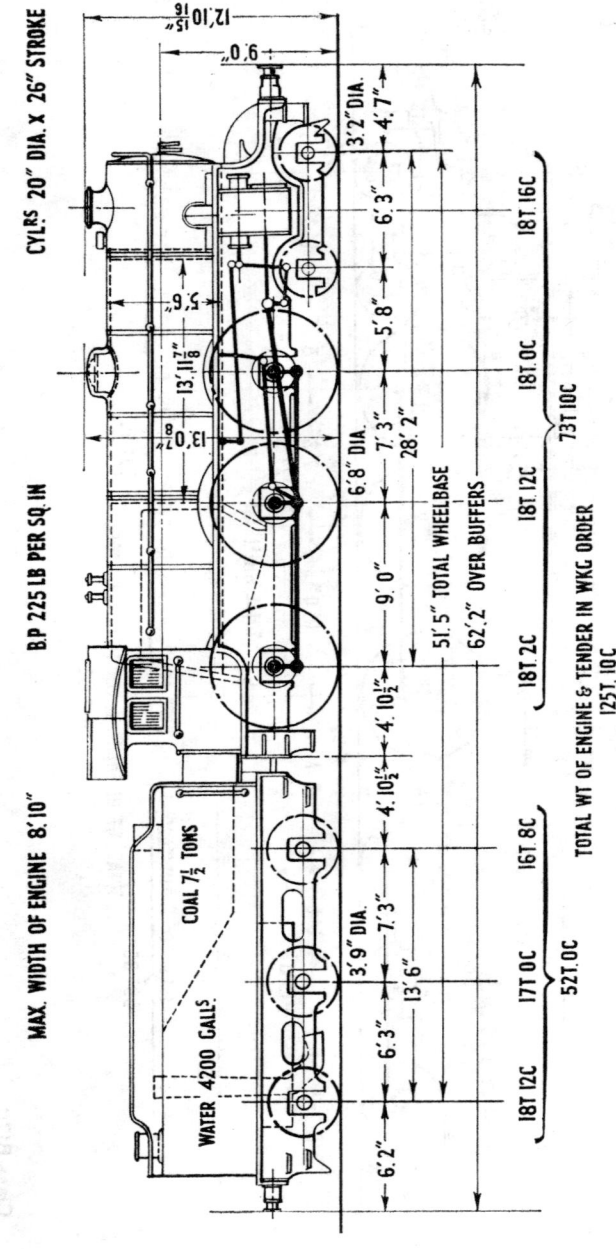

CYL.RS 20" DIA. X 26" STROKE

B.P 225 LB PER SQ IN

MAX. WIDTH OF ENGINE 8'10"

COAL 7½ TONS

WATER 4200 GALL.S

12'.10 15/16"

9'.0"

3'.2" DIA.

4'.7"

6'.3"

5'.6"

5'.8"

13'.11 7/8"

7'.3"

28' 2"

13'.0 7/8"

6'.8" DIA.

9'.0"

51' 5" TOTAL WHEELBASE

62'.2" OVER BUFFERS

4'.10½"

4'.10½"

3'.9" DIA.

7'.3"

13'.6"

6'.3"

6'.2"

18T.16C

18T.0C

73T.10C

18T.12C

18T.2C

16T.8C

17T.0C

18T.12C

52T.0C

TOTAL WT OF ENGINE & TENDER IN WKG ORDER
125T.10C

Class B2

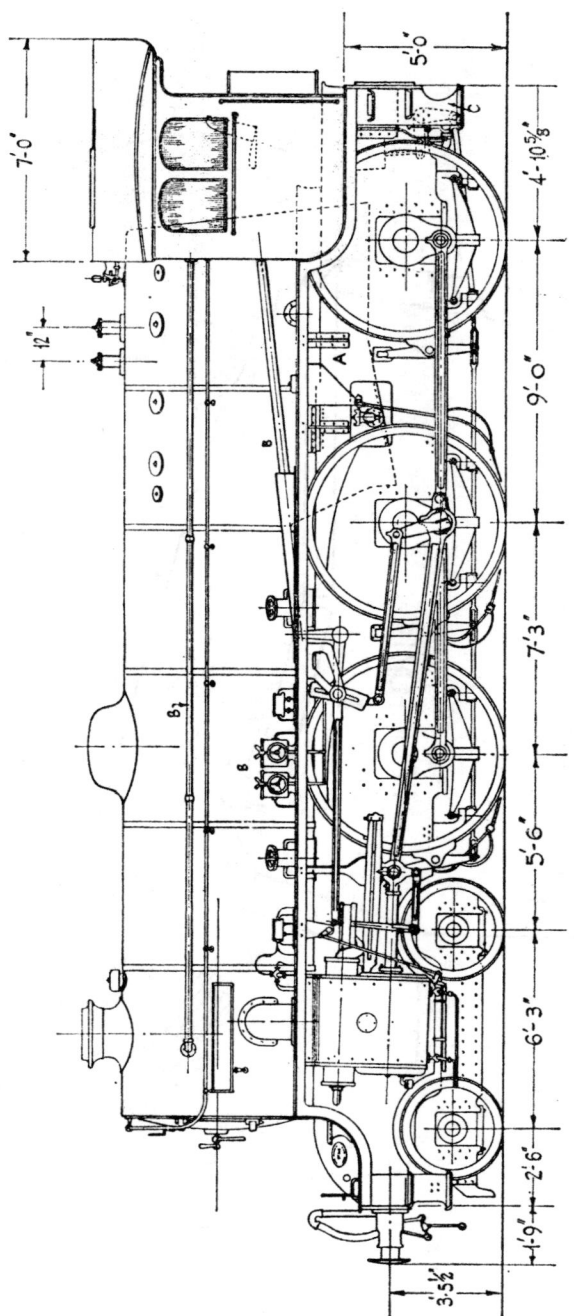

Class B1

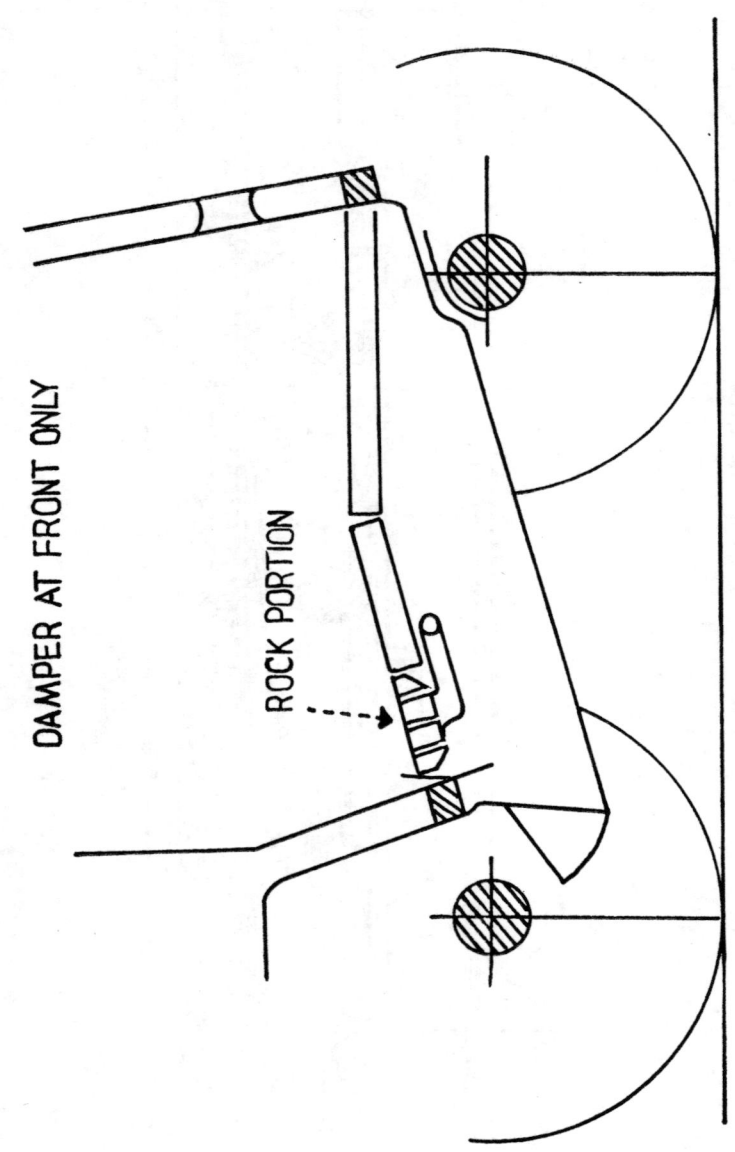

DAMPER AT FRONT ONLY

ROCK PORTION

CLASSES B1 & B17 FIREGRATE AND ASHPAN ARRANGEMENT

Bibliography

The Development of LNER Locomotive Design 1923–1941, B. Spencer. Paper read to The Institution of Locomotive Engineers, August 1947. Reprinted by the RCTS 1947.
Locomotive Performance and Efficiency Test Bulletins (Various issues) BTC.
Locomotives of the LNER, K. Prentice and P. Proud. RCTS 1941.
The Steam Locomotive in America, W. J. Bruce, W. W. Norton & Co 1952.
Locomotive Exchanges, Cecil J. Allen, Ian Allan 1949.
New Light on the Locomotive Exchanges, Cecil J. Allan, Ian Allan 1950.
Nigel Gresley Locomotive Engineer, F. A. S. Brown, Ian Allan 1961.
Locomotives of the LNER, A Preliminary Survey, Part 1, RCTS 1963.
World Steam in the 20th Century, E. S. Cox, Ian Allan 1969.
The London and North Eastern Railway, Cecil J. Allen, Ian Allan 1969.
Edward Thompson of the LNER, P. Grafton, Kestrel Books, 1971.
The Great Eastern Railway, Cecil J. Allen, Ian Allan 1955.
Great Central, Vol 3, George Dow, Ian Allan 1965.
Locomotives of the North Eastern Railway 1844–1922, E. S. MacLean. Loco. Pub. Co. 1923.
Locomotives of the North Eastern Railway, O. S. Nock, Ian Allan 1954.
Steam in the Blood, R. H. N. Hardy, Ian Allan 1971.
Great Central Steam, W. A. Tuplin, George Allen & Unwin 1967.
North Eastern Steam, W. A. Tuplin, George Allen & Unwin 1970.
Great Eastern Locomotives Past and Present, C. Langley Aldrich, Langloco Series 1944.
The Robinson Locomotives of the Great Central, C. Langley Aldrich, Langloco Series 1946.
From Inverness to Crewe, Martin Evans, Model Aeronautical Press Ltd, 1966.
Some Classic Locomotives, C. Hamilton Ellis, George Allen & Unwin 1949.
Twenty Locomotive Men, C. Hamilton Ellis, Ian Allan, 1958.
Chapelon, Genius of French Steam, Col. H. C. B. Rogers, Ian Allan 1972.
Various issues of:—
Railway Magazine, Railways, Railway World, Trains Illustrated, Modern Railways, The Railway Observer, The Journal of the Stephenson Locomotive Society, The Gresley Observer, The Leicester Railway Society Review, and the Ian Allan ABC Series.